Rise of
a Civilizational State

THE CHINA WAVE

RISE OF A CIVILIZATIONAL STATE

ZHANG WEIWEI

Fudan University & Chunqiu Institute
China

Geneva School of Diplomacy and International Relations
Switzerland

Published by

World Century Publishing Corporation

27 Warren Street, Suite 401-402, Hackensack, NJ 07601

Library of Congress Control Number: 2012932069

British Library Cataloguing-in-Publication Data
A catalogue record for this book is available from the British Library.

THE CHINA WAVE
Rise of a Civilizational State

Originally published in Chinese

Copyright © Horizon Media Co., Ltd., 2011

Copyright © 2012 by World Century Publishing Corporation

Published by arrangement with Shanghai Century Publishing Co. Ltd.
All Rights Reserved.

ISBN-13 978-1-938134-00-5
ISBN-10 1-938134-00-1
ISBN-13 978-1-938134-01-2 (pbk)
ISBN-10 1-938134-01-X (pbk)

In-house Editors: DONG Lixi
HO Yi Kai

Printed in Singapore by Markono Print Media Pte Ltd.

In memory of Deng Xiaoping (1904–1997) whose ideas have transformed China and inspired this book.

ACKNOWLEDGMENTS

This book is dedicated to all those who have contributed to China's dramatic rise, which has changed the lot of one-fifth of mankind forever, and to the visionary architect of this rise, China's late leader Deng Xiaoping, whom I had the privilege to serve as an English interpreter in the mid-1980s and whose many ideas have inspired me to write this book.

I owe an intellectual debt to many individuals and it is impossible to mention all of them, but I should thank those individuals, some of whom are also personal friends, who shared their perspectives with me on various issues discussed in the book. These individuals include Li Junru of the Central Party School; Eric Li, Jin Zhongwei and Sha Ye of the Chunqiu Institute; Shi Zhengfu, Chen Ping, Jiang Yihua and Xiao Sijian of Fudan University; Pan Wei of Beijing University; Zhang Wenmu of Beihang University; Wang Shaoguang of the Chinese University of Hong Kong; Wang Wen of the *Global Times*; Ji Guibao of the *Wenhui Daily*; Francis Fukuyama of Stanford University; and Robert Kuhn, the author of *How China's Leaders Think*.

I would like to express my special gratitude to K. K. Phua, Ho Yi Kai, Dong Lixi and their colleagues at World Scientific and World Century for their invaluable professional support in editing and publishing this book in English. My heartfelt thanks also go to Chen Xin, Hu Dawei, Shi Hongjun and Cai Xin of Shanghai Century Publishing for their dedicated professional assistance in editing and publishing the Chinese edition of the book. I should also thank Pan Xiaoli and H. B. Teng for their linguistic counsel, especially for Xiaoli's original proposal on the book's English title. I am most grateful to my wife Hui-Hui and my son Marco Yi-Zhou for their kind understanding and unfailing support.

I am alone, however, responsible for any errors that may appear in this book.

PREFACE TO THE ENGLISH EDITION

This book was written originally for Chinese readers, and it has become, quite unexpectedly, a bestseller in China since its first publication in January 2011, with perhaps a million copies sold, including pirated ones, in well under a year, which is rare for non-fiction books in China, and it topped the list of the ten most influential new books in China in 2011. A few reasons may explain its popularity.

First, China's extraordinary rise defies easy comprehension not only for foreigners, but also for the Chinese themselves, who have experienced first-hand the world's fastest economic and social transformation for three decades running, and many of them desire an independent, comprehensive and readable narrative about the meaning of this transformation for themselves and for their country.

Second, the Chinese are intensely curious about the outside world and about how their country compares with other countries after three decades of fast change, and they hope for an objective assessment of China's achievements, problems and future in comparison with other countries.

Third and perhaps more important, while the rest of the world is debating the rise of China and its global impact, China itself is engaged in a different type of debate, a highly heated one over the facts and nature of China's rise. It is perhaps not an exaggeration to claim that China's future

---

[1] The 2011 Shanghai Bookfair's List

may hinge on the result of this debate, as sharply different views represent different futures for China, and this book has become a centerpiece of this unfolding national debate.

The debate is gripped by two opposing views. One view holds that China is full of pitfalls and crises, and unless China follows the Western model, particularly the American one (despite the current crisis in the US), China will become a hopeless country. The other holds that whatever problems China has, the country is in its best shape in modern history, and China should continue to follow its own largely successful model of development while assimilating whatever is good from the outside, and if the model is abandoned China's future will be in tatters.

This book takes a clear position in favor of the latter view and argues that China's rise is not the rise of an ordinary country, but the rise of a country *sui generis*, a civilizational state, a new model of development and a new political discourse which questions many of the Western assumptions about democracy, good governance and human rights, and all this may well usher in a wave of change unprecedented in human history. The book also argues that the West may actually gain from China's rise in power and ideas, just as many developing or transitional economies have done.

As the book was originally meant for China's general public, not for international readers, its English edition entails more than mere translation, given the huge differences between the English and Chinese languages and between the vastly different cultures underpinning the linguistic divergences. I was courageous enough to undertake the difficult task of translating the book myself, as I thought this might ensure a more accurate rendition of my ideas contained in the book, but it soon occurred to me that this was indeed a daunting challenge: in addition to the due date set by my publisher, it was also an uphill struggle to render a book essentially for a Chinese audience into one for an international audience.

I have in the end adopted what can be called a 70/30 approach to completing this challenging task, i.e. roughly 70% of the work is to translate the original, in which I try to convey the meaning of the original text, style and tone, which are perhaps a bit sharp and provocative to those who are opposed to the China model, and the remaining 30% is essentially to rewrite or revise, partly to make the book more accessible to non-Chinese readers, and partly to share more material of particular interest to these readers. For instance, I have added more material on China's political reform and slightly simplified my discussions on comparing China with some individual countries in order to keep the book within a readable length.

I have also included my debate with Professor Francis Fukuyama, the author of *The end of History and the Last Man*, on the China model, which was held after the Chinese edition of the book had been published, and I use the verbatim record of this debate as the conclusion for the English edition, believing that the debate covers extensively the topics discussed in the book and touches on many issues of great interest to the international audience with an interest in the rise of China and its global implications.

As I have observed towards the end of the book, "China has learnt so much from the West and will continue to do so for its own benefit, and it may be time now for the West, to use Deng Xiaoping's famous phrase, to 'emancipate the mind' and learn a little more about or even from China's approach and the Chinese ideas, however extraneous they may appear, for its own benefit." This is not only to reduce further ideology-driven mis-readings of this hugely important nation, a civilization in itself, but also to enrich the world's collective wisdom in tackling challenges ranging from poverty eradication and the financial crisis to climate change and the clash of civilizations.

Zhang Weiwei
zhangweiweiyes@yahoo.com
Shanghai, November 30, 2011

CONTENTS

INTRODUCTION

As we know, China, or the rise of China, remains controversial in the West for all kinds of reasons. Indeed, over the past 30 or so years, the Chinese state has often been portrayed in the Western media as a dichotomy of a repressive regime clinging to power and a society led by pro-democracy dissidents bordering on rebellion, and some Europeans, for instance, in Oslo, still view China as an enlarged East Germany or Belarus awaiting a color revolution.

This perception has led many China-watchers in the West to confidently crystal-ball a pessimistic future for China: the regime would collapse after the Tiananmen event in 1989; China would follow in the footsteps of the Soviet Union in its disintegration; chaos would engulf China after Deng Xiaoping's death; the prosperity of Hong Kong would fade with its return to China; the explosion of SARS would be China's Chernobyl; China would fall apart after its WTO entry; and chaos would ensue following the 2008 global financial tsunami. Yet all these forecasts turned out to be wrong: it is not China that has collapsed, but all the forecasts about China's collapse that have "collapsed".

This unimpressive track record of crystal-balling China's future reminds us of the need to look at this huge and complex country in a more objective way, and perhaps with an approach adopted by the great German philosopher G. W. Leibniz (1646–1716) to focus on how the Chinese developed what he called "natural religion" or the secular application of ethics and political philosophy to social, economic and political governance. If we are freed from ideological hangups, we may come to see that what has happened over the past three decades in China is arguably the greatest economic and social revolution in human history: over 400 million people have been lifted out of poverty, with all the implications of this success for China and the rest of the world.

Interestingly, while China, following a model not endorsed by the West, stuns the world with its rapid reemergence, a sizable number of Chinese at home are not yet convinced. Some believers in the Western political and economic systems still hold that China will eventually fail if it is unwilling to follow the Western model. Yet no fair-minded person with a decent knowledge of world affairs today would turn a blind eye to China's rise. While the China model of development is by no means perfect, China's overall success is arguably unmatched by any developing or transitional economies that have copied the Western model, and this success has indeed taken most countries by surprise.

The China model has taken shape in the midst of global turbulence and competition. It is therefore resilient and competitive and unlikely to fall apart easily. With further improvements, the model's future is promising. From a long-term historical perspective, China's rise, at least to this author, is not that of an ordinary country, but the rise of a *civilizational state* (文明型国家).

This rise is unprecedented in human history. If the ancient civilizations of Egypt, Mesopotamia, the Indus Valley and Greece had continued till the present day and functioned within unified modern states, they would also be described as civilizational states. But this opportunity has been lost. If the ancient Roman Empire had stayed united till now and transformed into a modern state, Europe could also be a medium-sized civilizational state. But this is only a hypothesis. If dozens of countries of the Islamic world today could integrate into a unified modern state despite all their diverse traditions, it would also be a civilizational state with over 1 billion people. But this seems an unlikely prospect. Indeed, China is now the only country in the world which has amalgamated the world's longest continuous civilization with a huge modern state.

A civilizational state has exceedingly strong historical and cultural traditions. It does not easily imitate or follow other models, be they Western or otherwise. It has its own intrinsic logic of evolution and development. It is bound to encounter all kinds of challenges in the future, but its rise is seemingly unstoppable and irreversible. The civilizational state has a strong capability to draw on the strengths of other nations while maintaining its own identity. As an endogenous civilization capable of generating its own standards and values, it makes unique contributions to the world civilizations.

A civilizational state can exist and evolve independently of the endorsement or acknowledgment from others. Its political and economic models are different from others in many aspects. This was the case in the past, and is still so now and will remain so in the future, just as the expanding influence of the Chinese language does not require the endorsement of the English language, Sun Tzu's *The Art of War* does not need the stamp of approval of Clausewitz, Confucius does not need the acknowledgment of Plato, and China's current "macroeconomic regulation" does not need the approval of the US Federal Reserve Board.

What is more likely to happen is perhaps that the former may gradually influence the latter: the Chinese language will influence the evolution of the English language; *The Art of War* will continue to have an impact on the development of Western military thought; the thoughts of both Confucius and Plato will continue to provide valuable insights for mankind; and the Chinese approach to "macroeconomic regulation" may offer useful lessons to a country like the United States.

The first group of countries rising up in the world during the 18th and 19th centuries, like Britain and France, had a population of tens of millions; the second group of countries rising up during the 20th century, like the US and Japan, had a population of around 100 million; and China's rise in the 21st century represents a population of over one billion, which is more than the total population of the previous two groups. This is not merely a matter of the size of the population, but the rise of a different type of country, a country *sui generis*. It is the rise of a civilizational state, a new model of development and a new political discourse.

The world is thus witnessing a wave of change from a vertical world order, in which the West is above the rest in both wealth and ideas, to a more horizontal order, in which the rest, notably China, will be on a par with the West in both wealth and ideas. This is an unprecedented shift of economic and political gravity in human history, which will change the world forever.

CHAPTER 1

NOT MISREADING ONESELF

1.1 A Fast-Changing World

It is a fast-changing world. For quite a long time, China was unwilling to use the term "rise of China" to describe its rapid development for fear of arousing the rancor of the outside world, which, however, somehow favored the term. The Global Language Monitor, an American media research organization, conducted a search of the global print and digital media and the Internet at the end of 2009 and found that the rise of China was the top news item in the past decade, more than 9/11 or the Iraq War. It is true that the search focused on English-based materials and may not fully reflect the top news stories in the world. Yet, as English is the main medium of international communications today, the English-based search may indeed reflect the world's attention given to the rise of the world's most populous nation.

The speed of China's rise is stunning. China's total GDP has increased 18-fold since 1979 and the country is now the world's second-largest economy when its GDP is calculated in dollar terms at the official exchange rate. And if calculated in purchasing power parity (PPP), it is claimed that China may have already become the world's second-largest economy in 1992. The country also overtook Germany as the world's largest exporting country in 2009. Over the past three decades, US$800 billion worth of foreign investments have poured into China, and the country has become a locomotive for worldwide growth over the past few years. In 2009, it contributed to about 50% of the world's economic and trade growth. Lawrence H. Summers, former US Treasury Secretary, estimated that if a person's living standards doubled in his lifetime during Britain's Industrial Revolution, the living standards for a Chinese may increase seven times in his lifetime during China's process of modernization.

Up until ten years ago, the Western media had been lamenting the Chinese banking system for its excessive non-performing debts. But by 2010, three out of five of the world's largest banks were Chinese. Until five years ago, the G8's annual economic summit attracted worldwide attention. Now its function has been taken over by the G20. A year ago, some Western scholars were still predicting chaos in China due to the impact of the financial tsunami. Yet, China turned out to be the first country to emerge from the crisis and became the locomotive for the growth of the world economy.

Interestingly, although the rise of China is apparently acknowledged everywhere, some in China remain suspicious of or even hostile towards this fact. I recall that, having returned from a lecture tour in India at the end of 2008, I published a commentary titled "My Shock and Reflections on India's Slums" in a leading Chinese newspaper and then online. A reader left an interesting message for me: "Why compare China with India? Why not Eastern Europe?" I responded, "I've just visited Warsaw and Budapest recently. My impression is that they are about a decade behind Shanghai." Unconvinced, the reader then asked, "Warsaw and Budapest are nothing. Why not compare Shanghai with New York?" Comparing any Chinese mega-cities with New York was inconceivable 30 years ago, but it is now indeed worth doing. In fact, Thomas L. Friedman, the renowned *New York Times* columnist, has made such a comparison. Having attended the 2008 Summer Olympic Games in Beijing and visited Shanghai on his way back to New York, he published an interesting essay titled "A Biblical Seven Years" in *The New York Times* on August 27, 2008:

> As I sat in my seat at the Bird's Nest, watching thousands of Chinese dancers, drummers, singers and acrobats on stilts perform their magic at the closing ceremony, I couldn't help but reflect on how China and America have spent the last seven years: China has been preparing for the Olympics; we've been preparing for Al Qaeda. They've been building better stadiums, subways, airports, roads and parks. And we've been building

better metal detectors, armored Humvees and pilotless drones. The difference is starting to show. Just compare arriving at La Guardia's dumpy terminal in New York City and driving through the crumbling infrastructure into Manhattan with arriving at Shanghai's sleek airport and taking the 220-mile-per-hour magnetic levitation train, which uses electromagnetic propulsion instead of steel wheels and tracks, to get to town in a blink. Then ask yourself: Who is living in the third world country?

He continued,

Here's what's new: The rich parts of China, the modern parts of Beijing or Shanghai or Dalian, are now more state of the art than rich America. The buildings are architecturally more interesting, the wireless networks more sophisticated, the roads and trains more efficient and nicer. And, I repeat, they did not get all this by discovering oil. They got it by digging inside themselves.

Finally, he stated,

I never want to tell my girls that they have to go to China to see the future.

Friedman was probably too disappointed with George W. Bush and too frustrated with the fact that, misled by Bush, too much American money and time and too many American lives had been wasted in Iraq and Afghanistan. Indeed, China's mega-cities are still behind New York in one way or another. For example, Shanghai trails behind New York in international finance, urban cultural space and degree of internationalization. But in many other ways, Shanghai is now ahead or way ahead of New York. Shanghai's "hardware", such as airports, harbors, subways, highways, high-speed trains, skyscrapers and breath-taking night scenes, is better than New York's. Its "software", or important social indicators, such as street safety, infant mortality and life expectancy, is also better than New York's. Shanghai residents' sense of happiness may also be higher than that of the New Yorkers.

Of course, some people will say that China's mega-cities are indeed impressive but China's urban-rural disparity is huge. I tend to share this view, and China's urban-rural gap is greater than that in all the developed countries. Narrowing this gap will be China's next major task. But one should also be aware that in the process of modernization, the developed countries also grappled with the thorny issue of the urban-rural divide. Narrowing the gap will take time and can only be a gradual process, especially for a super-large country like China. Furthermore, although China's countryside still falls short of the standards of the developed countries, it has also been developing rapidly over the past three decades and, from my own observation, it is on the whole more developed than most developing countries in the world. I will further discuss this point in the next chapter.

Some people have questioned China's rise because of the perceived rise of corruption. Corruption is indeed serious in China today and calls for an earnest solution. But it is also true that from a historical perspective, the developed countries today, too, experienced rising corruption during their industrial revolutions. In the 19th century, the seats of the British parliament were up for sale; the American economy was then controlled by what historians called *robber barons*; and the family histories of the Carnegies and the Rockefellers were tarnished with blights. British historian Eric Hobsbawm revealed in his book *The Age of Capital: 1848–1875* that the US was then the most lawless place on earth, with rampant corruption and privately hired "police" executing criminals at will, and the US at the time did not have European-style government, so much so that the local people felt unsafe and had to rely on self-defense. The tradition of gun ownership in America started in that era. Japan's Meiji Restoration in the second half of the 19th century was also characterized by large-scale collusions between bureaucracy and businessmen. Many of Japan's major corporations today had been sold then at exorbitantly low prices to entrepreneurs with special ties to the state.

In his book *Political Order in Changing Societies,* American political scientist Samuel Huntington wrote, "Corruption may be more prevalent in some cultures than in others but in most cultures it seems to be most prevalent during the most intense phases of modernization." Why does corruption increase with the pace of modernization? The principal reason is that the rule of law and state supervision can hardly catch up with the fast expansion of wealth. This is unfortunately common with the rise of all major powers and will take time to resolve.

Moreover, even if the old type of corruption is brought under control, new types may well emerge. The 2008 financial tsunami has presented much of what I call "the second generation of corruption" in the US. Wall Street's financial frauds, especially regulatory arbitrage, were shocking and brought havoc to the world. And indeed, fighting corruption is a long-term process and its significant reduction requires the rule of law as well as the economic, social and educational development of a society.

From a comparative perspective, the annual reports compiled by Transparency International, an authoritative international organization in the field of corruption study, and my own field observations seem to reveal that those comparable developing countries or transitional economies, for example, with a population above 50 million, tend to have more corruption than China, as shown in the Philippines, Thailand, Bangladesh, India, Pakistan, Brazil, Egypt, Indonesia, Ukraine and Russia, all of which have adopted some form of the Western political system, not to mention the many so-called democracies with endemic corruption in Africa.

Is China's rise real if its environmental degradation is so serious? Indeed, environmental protection is another challenge for China but one should not be excessively discouraged. In the history of its industrialization Europe experienced perhaps more pollution than China today. For instance, it was reported that in 1952 more than 4,000 people died of coal-smoke pollution in London in a week. The Rhine River was once pronounced biologically dead as fish died and swimming became impossible. But Europe eventually brought the issue under control with its large-scale ecological protection programs and now leads the world in environmental protection. With a firm commitment to promoting environmental protection, China may well eventually catch up, as the strength of the China model lies in the fact that once consensus is reached and the goals are set out, the China model acts far more efficiently than the Western model, as shown in the way China is moving ahead in developing renewable energy: in the space of a few years, China is now leading the world in wind and solar energy and in the electric car industry.

Is China's rise real when the gap between the rich and poor is huge, with a Gini coefficient of 0.45 or even 0.47? Indeed, this gap is certainly bigger than ever before in China's history and it is now a thorny issue to be handled with determination and care. Besides the gap itself, China has an exceedingly strong cultural tradition of "fearing not insufficiency but unequal distribution", and China's development will be hampered if this issue is not tackled well. Yet, with all this, one still needs to look at the issue as it is. For instance, the often-cited Gini coefficient is based on monetized income difference and neglects the value of the land and properties held by China's perceived poor, especially farmers in China. In comparison, most developing countries have never experienced genuine land reforms, so their poor have neither land nor housing, and are indeed far poorer than their Chinese counterparts, who have both land and private housing thanks to the country's land reform. If the Gini coefficient took into account the value of land and properties owned by the Chinese farmers, it would be significantly different.

China's rich-poor divide is relative, and even the low-income group lives a better life today than ever before while the high-income earners see their wealth increase faster. The nature of the issue facing China today is different from that of absolute poverty in most developing countries. According to statistics published by the World Bank, nearly 70% of the world's poverty reduction over the past 20 years was achieved in China.[1]

Indeed, you could drive 20 hours from downtown Beijing or Shanghai in any direction, so long as you don't drive into the sea or cross the borders, and expect to see many villages, towns and cities. But all the poverty you see along the way in China may be less than what you could expect to see if you drive for two hours from the city center of India's Mumbai, Pakistan's Karachi, Nigeria's Lagos or Egypt's Cairo, where you will see so much of the extreme poverty which has already been eradicated from China: slums thriving with hundreds of thousands of the poor and countless impoverished homeless people. The number of the extremely impoverished has declined drastically in China with three decades of reform since 1978. But most other developing countries remain far from reaching this goal.

Is China's rise real if its housing prices are so exorbitantly high that college graduates cannot afford an apartment or even a marital home? But

---

[1] See the website of the International Poverty Reduction Center in China: http://www.iprcc. org.cn/front/article/article.action?id=2037.

anyone with a slight knowledge of the housing situations elsewhere in the world would know that China may well be one of the very few countries where young college graduates in their mid-20s can consider buying homes and a girl can openly list home ownership as a pre-condition for marriage. Frankly, none of the developed countries have reached this standard. A popular TV serial, *Woju* (*Dwelling Narrowness*), shows people's helplessness with regard to the rising housing prices in China, and the female lead laments to her husband, "If we add up both of our ages, it's nearly 70, but we still don't even have our own apartment." To be honest, this kind of lament would be rare in a developed country like Switzerland, where the home ownership is about 36% and it is simply unrealistic for most of the Swiss to own a home in their early 30s. Most couples in developed countries get married in rental properties, and indeed, the housing demand in China seems to exceed that in the developed countries. This fact serves to illustrate the swift pace with which China is catching up with or even surpassing the developed countries in various aspects.

Nevertheless, some international practices are worth considering. For instance, most people may consider renting first and purchasing later when they have enough savings. Obviously, the rental market needs better regulation in China. At the same time, one should encourage innovative approaches to solve the housing issue as the Chinese have the world's strongest tradition of home ownership. For example, we may consider combining home renting and purchasing. The renter can purchase the house at a preferential price after renting it for a certain number of years. We can also draw on the experience of China's 1998 housing reform to start a "minimum housing program" (such as selling minimum-size apartments to qualified young families at the construction cost and with certain conditions attached). Thus, China will see, on a greater scale, the rise of the world's largest property-owning class. As the saying goes, those with properties desire stability, and home ownership will be in China's long-term interest in maintaining stability and creating a consumption-driven economy.

China is still faced with many difficulties and challenges. It is not easy to achieve full modernization in a country with a massive population and a vast territory like China. But China has done well in poverty eradication and modernization over the past 30 or so years. China is unwilling to proclaim its rise, but its rise has been well noted. It prefers to keep a low profile in world affairs, yet it has done quite a lot on the world stage. Its currency, the *RMB*, is in theory not freely convertible, but in reality it can be exchanged in many parts of the world today. It claims to be a developing country but fewer and fewer people outside China take this claim seriously. China is unwilling to use the concept of the China model but the rest of the world uses it extensively in discussions on China. China, with a long-term vision, is determinedly modest, yet regardless of this modesty, China's rise is indeed stunning to the outside world by any standard.

1.2 The Unusual Ascent

The most impressive characteristic of China's rise is its peaceful nature, with internal stability and unity, without resorting to wars against other countries as with the rise of Western powers in the past. This is perhaps a miracle in human history. World history shows that the rise of the West was associated with turmoil and wars. Take the mid to late 19th century as an example, when Europe and the US experienced industrial revolutions. The British launched the Opium War against China in 1839, and the entire Europe was engulfed by revolutions and chaos in 1848. By the second half of the 19th century, major Western countries such as Britain and France had carved up Africa, and conflicts between the Western powers were rife in their colonies. Beyond Africa, the Crimean War broke out between Britain, France, Turkey and Russia in 1853. France invaded Indochina in 1858 and took full control of it in 1865. Britain and France launched the Second Opium War against China in 1856, occupied Beijing and plundered and burnt down the Old Summer Palace. In 1860, France entered Syria and intervened in Mexico by propping up a pro-French emperor (1861–1867). At the same time, Italy achieved national unity (1859–1870) amidst bloodshed. France cracked down on the Paris Commune in 1871. Germany was unified by the "blood and iron" Chancellor Bismarck following the Franco-Prussian War (1870–1871) and the defeat of the Second French Empire.

The American victory in the Mexican-American War (1846–1848) brought large tracts of land and resources, including California, under its control. The American Civil War broke out in 1861 and 630,000 soldiers died (30–40% of the total forces). Britain lurked in the shadows of the Civil War because the South's slavery-based agriculture had supplied raw materials for Britain's industries. From this perspective, the Civil War was also an American domestic war to end American dependence on Britain. After the Civil War, the massacre of native Indians started in 1867 when Congress passed a bill to expel the Indians and establish Indian settlements. The Americans started to migrate to the prairie lands west of the Mississippi River. By 1883, 15 years after the passing of the bill, an untold number of Indians had been killed and the US acquired free access to huge amounts of land and natural resources. The destiny of the Chinese in the US was also miserable. The Chinese made up a third of Idaho's population in 1870, and they helped build the cross-continental railways but, like the African Americans, they had neither land nor freedom. The freedom of the cowboys belonged to the white men who were mostly poor migrants from Europe.

Some Chinese scholars today are reluctant to mention the wars and bloodshed throughout the rise of the West, which most Western scholars themselves do not deny. This is perplexing, as most of the Chinese today understand the meaning of "the first pot of gold" for an individual's wealth accumulation after 30 years of reform and opening up. The "first pot of gold" for the rise of the West came with wars and bloodshed. There are unfortunately mining incidents in some parts of China, and the wealth generated from the mining industry is sometimes described in the Chinese media as "blood-tainted GDP". If this analogy holds, the GDP generated during the rise of the Western powers may well be described as "blood-soaked GDP".

The rise of China is not the rise of another ordinary country but the rise of one fifth of the world's population. It is the rise of a civilizational state with a long history and a vast territory. Many of the issues it is faced with today once occurred in the times of the Western emergence. During Europe's industrial revolutions, there were huge rich-poor divides, social injustice, rampant corruption and violent plundering. But compared to China today, the Western powers could "solve" their problems then with relative ease. For example, Britain could "export" its criminals to Australia, its unemployed to Africa and its heretics to America. It could make all the world's political and economic "rules of the game", and it did not matter much when the rich-poor gap was several dozen times larger than China's today as the practice of engaging millions of slaves and coolies was considered legal.

In comparison, China today has to solve, on its own soil, all the issues brought about by industrialization, modernization and their associated social shifts. When Britain ushered in the Industrial Revolution in the 18th century, its population was around 10 million, smaller than that in any of China's major cities today. When France was undergoing the process of industrialization in the 19th century, its population was around 20 million, but China today is already a nation of 1.3 billion people. It is carrying out large-scale industrial and social revolutions under very unfavorable conditions. It has to resolve all its problems internally without resorting to wars, and it does not plunder other countries. In fact, its rise has bought far more tangible benefits to both China and the world at large, as the country has become the engine of the world's economic growth. From this perspective, China's success and the model underpinning its success are significant and invaluable. With their diligence, sacrifice and wisdom, the Chinese have created a miracle and pioneered their own model of development, thus preparing China to tackle other challenges in the years to come and opening up broad vistas for China's future.

1.3 Surpassing Japan

In 2010, China's total GDP surpassed Japan's, and this news attracted worldwide attention. The Western media immediately published a good many comments. *The Times* of the UK highlighted the fact that China's leap to the second place in the world signaled a major shift in the global economic and political power. *The New York Times* called it the "milestone" in China's progress and "though anticipated for some time, it's the most striking evidence yet that China's ascendance is for real and that the rest of the world will have to reckon with a new economic superpower". The French daily *Figaro* commented that the people's long anticipation had become a reality, and this trend of change would continue. Now, most mainstream Western economists predict that the Chinese economy may overtake the US in 10 to 20 years.

In comparison, the Chinese media is rather muted. Most of them stress that China is still a developing country and its GDP per capita is only one tenth of Japan's, so being the second-largest economy in the world does not mean much. From my point of view, this low-key approach is adopted by two groups of people. The first group prefers to be modest and cautious, in line with Deng Xiaoping's policy of "keeping a low profile". They see more the gaps between China and the developed countries in many areas and are concerned that the high GDP estimate could entail unnecessarily heavy international burdens for China. The second group is different, as it consists of those who simply do not see or are unwilling to acknowledge China's rapid development. They try to play down the significance of China surpassing Japan and even cite the case of China's failure in the Opium War of 1839–1840, when China was the world's largest economy and yet lost the war to the British.

But my understanding is that, whether it is the Chinese modesty to keep a low profile or not, China itself should be able to assess objectively the real China and its economic power. If "keeping a low profile" means to disparage oneself at will, it may eventually lead to a situation where the Chinese lose confidence in their country and in China's own model of development. This is also dangerous. In fact, those who do not want to see the China model succeed often mislead the people this way, and they have succeeded in shaping a kind of mean-spirited passivity among a sizable Chinese population. To reverse this trend, one should tell the truth to the people about China's rise. Over the past 20 years, I have visited more than 100 countries and China is undoubtedly the country where the fastest overall progress has been made and where people's living standards see the most tangible improvements. China is tackling the same type of problems which other powers had encountered in the past and resolved in the process of development. It is necessary to base ourselves on this new understanding and shape a new national consensus on China's path of development. We should "keep a low profile" but it should be based on self-confidence, self-respect and self-strength, rather than on low-spirited passivity. This will allow us to meet the internal and external challenges more effectively and to open up new prospects for China's future.

From my point of view, all statistics and rankings for China, especially in terms of per capita GDP, will change significantly if two factors are introduced into the equation. The first is purchasing power parity (PPP), i.e. if we calculate on the basis of PPP, rather than the official exchange rate. This is a common sense approach as, for instance, a similar meal in Japan's restaurants is usually ten times more expensive than in Beijing or Shanghai. It follows that the Japanese restaurants will generate ten times more GDP when preparing a similar meal than in Beijing or Shanghai if the calculation is based on the official exchange rate. The error will naturally snowball. Generally speaking, the PPP estimates are relatively more reliable, and it has been increasingly used among the academia for international comparisons. Angus Maddison, a noted British economic historian, researched the PPP-adjusted GDP and came to the conclusion that China's economy in fact surpassed Japan's in 1992 and then surpassed the combined GDP of 12 major European industrialized countries, including Germany, Britain and France, in 2009. He reasoned that the Chinese economy would surpass that of the US in 2015[2] and I will further elaborate on the PPP issue in the next chapter.

Irrespective of China using PPP or not, the CIA has always assessed China's strength based on PPP. The Americans' talk of the G2 is not entirely unfounded. It is China's rapid rise that the US has to come to terms with. It did not propose the idea of a G2 to Russia or India, not even Europe, but to China. This is because without China's cooperation, the US cannot solve any of the thorny issues it is faced with today. But China is unlikely to enjoy policing the world together with the US, as doing so, from a Chinese point of view, tends to make enemies around the world and, furthermore, this does not fit the Chinese mentality or Chinese way of behaving.

The second factor is home ownership. Chinese have arguably the world's strongest tradition of property ownership and hence one of the world's highest rates of home ownership. It is only fair to refer to another indicator, i.e., the household median net worth, for international comparisons, because it may reflect more accurately the real living standards of the people than per capita GDP. Household net worth refers to the total assets of a household, including properties, savings and stocks, less its total debts. A report titled "How to Gauge Your Middle-Class Status",

---

[2]《二十一世纪经济导报》 (21st Century Business Herald), August 1, 2009.

published in March 2010 in *US News and World Report*, reveals that "the typical American household has a net worth of \$84,000" after the financial crisis.[3] The statistics published by the Federal Reserve in March 2010 show that the total assets of the American household shrank roughly by 25% to the level of 2004 due to the crisis. That year, the median net worth of the American household was US\$93,000.[4]

Based on the exchange rate of US\$1 to 6.37 *yuan*, US\$84,000 is roughly 535,000 *yuan*, and US\$93,000 is about 593,000 *yuan*. Even at its peak in 2007 when the American household median net worth was around US\$150,000, or nearly 1 million *yuan*, how many Chinese households today have the median net worth of 535,000 and 593,000 *yuan*? How many have reached 1 million *yuan*? I do not yet have authoritative data on this, but my estimate is that there are perhaps already 100 million or so households (or one quarter of Chinese households) with a net worth of between 535,000 and 593,000 *yuan*. The speed of wealth creation in China over the past three decades is unparalleled in human history.

It is no secret that the Americans are more used to credit consumption and have thus become the world's largest consumer market over the past few decades. But this is also a major cause of the current financial crisis, and it reminds us of the need not to imitate the American practice of excessive credit consumption. Yet, it is my considered view that if China can develop a moderate level of credit consumption, especially based on the enormous Chinese household assets, China will gradually become the world's largest consumer market.

As for China's defeat in the 1839–1840 Opium War despite its GDP being the world's largest, this was mainly because China was still not yet a modern state, but a traditional state, loosely held together by a weak central government like a pile of sand, whereas Britain was already a modern nation-state with a modern economy, strong national cohesion and an unmatched power for war mobilization. Suppose that a province of China then had been able to reach approximately the level of a modern nation-state, say Guangdong province, with a level of industry and trade like that of the British, then the Opium War could have been avoided, as it meant

---

[3] "How to Gauge Your Middle-Class Status", *US News and World Report*, March 23, 2010.
[4] Federal Reserve Board, Survey of Consumer Finances, March 2010.

that the province would have substantial capabilities for modern state governance, industry, foreign trade, defense and diplomacy, and Britain would have been deterred by all this. The situation in China today is different. In fact, back in the early 1950s, China and Britain already engaged each other on the battlefield during the Korean War and the British had a hard time, as shown by the fate of the Royal Scots.

Furthermore, we should look a little deeper into history, especially at how Japan completed its capital accumulation for modernization. Otherwise, it will be difficult to appreciate the significance of China's peaceful rise. In the 19th century, China was one step behind Japan in embracing modernization and it ended up being attacked and ransacked by foreign powers. After the success of the Meiji Restoration in the second half of the 19th century, Japan joined the ranks of the Western powers and started the Sino-Japanese War in 1894. After the defeat of China, Japan extorted an indemnity of 230 million taels of silver from China. What did 230 million taels of silver mean? It was roughly equivalent to three years of China's state revenue then. Japan spent it on improving education, setting up factories, constructing cities and expanding the army. Japan's overall economic and military power thus increased rapidly. How much Chinese sweat, money and resources did the Japanese extort for its modernization? How many Chinese lives had been lost due to Japan's invasion of China? Too numerous to count. In comparison, foreign invasions, the outflow of silver and an empty treasury pushed China towards a spiral of sharp decline. By 1900, it was invaded by the Eight-Nation Alliance and was forced to pay an indemnity of 450 million taels of silver, and then China became indeed the "sick man of East Asia". In China's modern history, China's economic development was relatively fast and its national strength was on the increase prior to the Sino-Japanese War of 1894–1895 and the Mukden Incident of 1931. However, the two wars launched by Japan abruptly ended China's modernization drive and caused the Chinese economy to backslide by decades and tens of millions of lives to be lost. China had to start again from scratch in 1949. After several decades of unremitting efforts and rapid and peaceful development, China has finally made huge strides and overtaken Japan to become the world's second-largest economy. Indeed, from my point of view China overtaking Japan is a milestone in world affairs with long-term implications for the future of China and the rest of the world.

1.4 The GDP Paradox

We have an interesting GDP complex, and it is therefore necessary to elaborate a bit on the concept of GDP. China is often in an awkward position. When one talks about China's progress, one refers to the fact that the Chinese economy is already the second-largest in the world. But China is also described as a developing country, with a per capita GDP as low as that of Albania, according to the official exchange rate, which ranks China around the 100th in the world. However, I visited the Albanian capital of Tirana and its port city Durrës five years ago and their level of development and prosperity was much lower than that of any medium-sized coastal cities in China. At this stage of China's development, it is necessary to present a clear and honest account of the concept of GDP, especially that of per capita GDP.

I have a per capita GDP-related anecdote. During a tour of Lagos, the biggest city of Nigeria, in April 2008, I met a Chinese businessman who had just returned from Equatorial Guinea, one of the smallest African countries. We chatted, and I asked him which country was more developed, Equatorial Guinea or Nigeria. "Of course, it's Nigeria," he replied without any hesitancy. Curious, I asked, "How is it possible? The per capita GDP in Equatorial Guinea is about US$20,000 whereas in Nigeria it's about US$2,000." He explained, "No matter how dilapidated Lagos is, there's at least running water in town, but there's no running water in most areas in the capital of Equatorial Guinea, and a sewage system doesn't exist either." He claimed, "The worst is malaria. All Chinese who have lived in Equatorial Guinea, including successive Chinese ambassadors, have fallen victim to malaria one after another." He then went on to describe the horror of African malaria, "High fever, body pain, your head feels like exploding, and you really want to bang your head on the wall." From my observation, Lagos is about 30 years behind Beijing in terms of modernization. If what the Chinese businessman said is true, the situation in Equatorial Guinea could be pretty miserable. But Beijing's GDP per capita in 2009 was about US$10,000 whereas that of Equatorial Guinea was double Beijing's. How to make sense of this paradox? The reason is not complicated. Equatorial Guinea discovered oil reserves in the mid-1970s but the reserves were controlled by the president and his close relatives. Later, foreign corporations came in to develop the oil fields, and instantly this poor country attained a per capita GDP of US$20,000. It became "rich" overnight from the oil reserves but this wealth did not bring running water, a sewage system, employment or the formation of a middle class to the people. The country's wealth is controlled by a few people and its per capita GDP has nothing to do with the lives of the ordinary people.

I could draw an analogy here: suppose that Beijing's Chaoyang district has the highest per capita GDP while Beijing's Yanqing county the lowest. But one day, huge gold reserves are discovered in Yanqing which in turn attract large investors. As the population of Yanqing is much smaller than that of Chaoyang, its per capita GDP may surpass that of Chaoyang district overnight. It is therefore necessary to consider various factors such as the levels of economic development, education, healthcare, housing and average life span when we measure the level of development and the quality of life in a given place.

In comparison, the UN Human Development Index (HDI) is more accurate, as it takes into consideration some social indicators. But it is also problematic as, for instance, it gives undue weight to per capita GDP and excludes housing and home ownership, and housing is the largest asset for the Chinese. Hence, HDI may not be that accurate for China either.

In the summer of 2009, I attended an international seminar held by the UN Human Development Report Office (HDRO) in Geneva where many participants criticized the computation of HDI. The Russian representative suggested that the data used must be unbiased and the compilation process be more transparent. The Moroccan representative argued that the current ranking system was unscientific, and he proposed to categorize countries on a comparable basis before comparing them. He said, for example, that comparing a resource-scarce country with a resource-rich country did not explain anything. The Iranian representative suggested designing a development index which would take account of the impact of external factors on a country such as the financial crisis, food crisis and fuel crisis. The Chinese representative observed that "greater caution should be exercised when introducing those indexes and computational methods which are viewed as immature or controversial, and more focus should be given to the growing knowledge and experience of development in developing countries and to reflecting the various development challenges faced by humanity". The director of the HDRO present acknowledged the controversies over the HDI which, he agreed, should be further improved in the future. In other words, even with regard to the index systems developed and used by international organizations, one should adopt an attitude of "seeking truth from facts" and apply them with necessary caution. Chinese scholars should be encouraged to make their original contributions to the shaping of new and more objective index systems.

In addition, it is necessary to understand the two main methods for computing GDP. One is based on the official exchange rate and the other on PPP. Most of our statistics are based on the former, but I tend to think that the latter is more accurate. International consensus seems to be that the current official exchange rate has underestimated the actual purchasing power of the RMB, and the PPP method may better reflect the reality of the Chinese economy. I have already cited the example of comparing meals in Japanese restaurants which cost ten times more than in Chinese restaurants. I can also use the cost of haircuts in Europe to make a comparison. A boy's simple haircut costs 20 euros in Europe, but only 20 *yuan* in China's most expensive cities like Beijing and Shanghai. According to the official exchange rate at the beginning of 2009, 1 euro equaled roughly 10 *yuan*, so a boy's haircut in Europe would be 200 *yuan*; in other words, it would generate ten times more GDP than in China. This is just an example to illustrate how the GDP based on the official exchange rate may grossly underestimate the real size of the Chinese economy.

As this is the case, more and more international institutions have started to use the PPP method, which is to compute the actual domestic purchasing power of a currency through comparing the prices of a basket of goods and services, as a way to correct the possible distortions in the official exchange rate method. But it does not mean that the PPP method can always guarantee a perfect comparison, as, for instance, the quality of comparable goods and services is difficult to measure. But on the whole, the PPP method is apparently more accurate than the official exchange rate method. In the years to come, it will be perhaps advisable for China to publish its GDP figures compiled in both methods. This will help the Chinese and non-Chinese to understand more accurately the world's second-largest economy.

I do not mind the continued use of the official exchange rate method in certain situations. It may be helpful in keeping our tradition of staying low-key and working hard. But I also maintain the view that the Chinese should acquire a real knowledge of their country's strength, neither exaggerated nor underestimated, and this is also to provide a more convincing account of China both at home and abroad.

The use of the PPP method also serves to correct some statistical distortions and prevent our own possible mistakes in decision-making. For example, China's foreign trade, based on the official exchange rate, accounts for 60–70% of China's GDP. This is obviously untrue, as it inflates the weight of foreign trade in the Chinese economy. It is true that China's export-oriented economy led to the rapid growth of China's foreign trade dependency, but the dependency cannot be that high. The confusion lies in the fact that the foreign trade data is calculated in US dollars, while the rest of China's GDP in the undervalued RMB, thus exaggerating China's foreign trade dependency in the Chinese economy.

Using the PPP method may also prevent a misreading of China and avoid geopolitical crises. For instance, Angus Maddison noted that the last governor of Hong Kong, Chris Patten, wrongly estimated China's strength, which probably caused him to provoke China over Hong Kong's political reform. Patten observed in the *Economist* in 1997 that Britain's GDP was nearly twice that of China, and China's GDP equaled the total GDP of Belgium, the Netherlands and Luxembourg. But according to Maddison's PPP-adjusted computation, Britain's GDP was then a third of China's. China's GDP was 6.5 times the total of Belgium, the Netherlands and Luxembourg.

It is expected that the PPP method will be used more often by the international statistics community as it is on the whole more accurate, and Chinese social scientists should look beyond the mainstream Western indexes currently in use, including those used by international organizations. Chinese scholars should, in the spirit of "seeking truth from facts", develop on their own initiative some more accurate and objective index systems as a way to shape international standards for cross-country comparisons.

As mentioned earlier, any measurement or ranking of the Chinese wealth will change significantly if two more factors are incorporated. One is the actual purchasing power of the Chinese currency. The other is home ownership. Housing usually accounts for about 60% of the net household assets for a typical Chinese family, so no international comparison of living standards will hold if it fails to reflect this fact. Take the comparison of Shanghai and Switzerland as an example. The Swiss home ownership is about 36% whereas it is about 75% in Shanghai. Many Shanghai residents own more than one property. Even though the Swiss nominal GDP is five times higher than that of Shanghai, its food and many daily expenses are five to ten times more expensive than in Shanghai, and Swiss home ownership is only half of Shanghai's. Hence, the wealth or even living standards of many Shanghai residents are higher than the average Swiss.

Life expectancy is another major indicator of the status of development. In China's mega-cities such as Beijing and Shanghai, the average life expectancy is over 80, higher than that in New York. This is the standard for a developed country. All these highlight the need to establish a more accurate and objective index system to reflect the real China and the real world. This should be an important part of China's efforts to build up its soft power, and China's social scientists have a lot to do in this field.

If GDP reflects more of a quantitative change, qualitative changes have also taken place in China. An editorial published in *Joongang*, a major South Korean daily, in February 2010 titled "China's Huawei Phenomenon" presented a unique perspective on China's quantitative to qualitative change:

> At the end of last year, a story out of the Swedish capital of Stockholm stuns the Western IT industry. The Chinese telecom provider, Huawei, won the bid to construct the 4G telecom network in Sweden, as Ericsson, the world's leading telecom company, is headquartered in Sweden. A Chinese company can defeat a Swedish one with perhaps the best telecom technologies in the world in his home terrain? The telecom industry was indeed surprised. Actually, it is nothing surprising, and Huawei's technology is as good as its competitor, and Huawei's rise is expected, and even the term "Huawei phenomenon" has been coined to reflect this trend. As a matter of fact, besides the IT industry, China's world class companies also include BYD, an electric car company, the Cord Blood Corporation listed on New York Stock Exchange and Suntech Power, a

leader in solar energy industry. The Huawei phenomenon is also reflected in the high-speed rail between Wuhan and Guangzhou, which averages 350 km per hour, faster than that in Germany, Japan and France. Witnessing China's rapid technological development, "How can all this be possible in a matter of ten years?" the industry wondered. There is a secret to China's super leap. China does not simply try to catch up with the technology of the developed countries. Rather it bypasses three or four stages of technological development and reaches directly the level of the developed country. It trades domestic market for technologies, and transplants the advanced technologies to Chinese industries. Experts tend to believe that China has made the leap in major industries such as automobile, shipbuilding, steel and iron and aviation industries.

The editorial asserted:

Fundamentally speaking, all these are made possible thanks to the state leadership. China's investment in R&D grows around 20% each year over a decade, and the government has endeavoured to attract overseas talents. Chinese enterprises have also responded positively to the relevant state policies. The joint efforts of state and enterprises in technological development have produced the Swedish impact. There is perhaps a "Huawei" in every line of Chinese industries. Nevertheless, South Korea's understanding of China still remains at the level of "producer of the fake and inferior." Only by changing the way we understand China can we really understand China as it is.[5]

It is fair to say that China's real strength lies in its rapid progress in both qualitative and quantitative terms.

1.5 To the Top

Angus Maddison's surveys, perhaps the largest PPP-based comparative studies of the world economies up to now, contain several interesting findings: the Chinese economy overtook Japan's in 1992 and surpassed the combined GDP of the 12 major industrialized countries in Europe in

---

[5] *Joongang*, February 8, 2010.

2009, namely, Britain, Switzerland, Sweden, Norway, Finland, Italy, Germany, France, the Netherlands, Denmark, Belgium and Austria. It is expected to surpass the US around 2015, and by 2030 it may well be an economy 1.13 times larger than the US. This reminds many Chinese of a famous observation made by Chairman Mao in 1956:

> You have such a big population, such a vast territory and such rich resources, and what's more, you're said to be building socialism, which is supposed to be superior. Yet if after practicing it for fifty or sixty years, you're still unable to overtake the United States, what a sorry figure you will cut yourself! You should be read off the face of the earth. Therefore, to overtake the United States is not only possible, but very necessary and obligatory. If we don't, the Chinese nation will let the nations of the world down and we will not make much of a contribution to mankind.[6]

Maddison's prediction seems to tally well with Mao's forecast back in 1956. PricewaterhouseCoopers' 2010 report forecasted that China would surpass the US to become the world's largest economy in 2020. In 2003, Goldman Sachs predicted that the Chinese GDP would be on a par with the US by 2041, but five years later in 2008, this was revised from 2041 to 2027. Robert Fogel, Nobel laureate in economics and professor at the University of Chicago, is the most sanguine about China's future. He predicted in an article carried in *Foreign Policy* in 2010 that the Chinese economy would reach US$123 trillion by 2040, or 40% of the global GDP, and dwarf that of the United States (14%). Furthermore, China's per capita income would hit US$85,000, more than double the forecast for the European Union, and also much higher than that of Japan but still behind the US. He wrote, "This is what the future will look like in 20 to 30 years. It's coming sooner than we have expected." Why is Fogel so optimistic? He reasoned that the forecast on China should consider the quantitative changes as well as the qualitative changes. He argued that China has entered a phase of large-scale urbanization, and "the productivity of an industrial worker is five times that of an agricultural worker, as shifting a

---

[6] Mao Zedong, *Mao Zedong Wenji* (Collected Works of Mao Zedong), Vol. 7, p. 80, People's Press, Beijing, 1999.

labourer from countryside to cities will create five times more productivity". It is still difficult to assess Fogel's forecast, but back in 1999 he had
predicted that China's annual automobile production would reach 10 million by 2015, and he was more optimistic than most other economists, at
a time when China's annual automobile production capacity was only
around 500,000. It was later proven that by 2009, China had already
become the world's largest auto market with annual sales at 13.5 million
cars.

In August 2010, Klaus Schwab, Executive Chairman of the World
Economic Forum, estimated that by 2015, the US share of the global GDP
would be 18.3% whereas China's would be 16.9%. Wang Tao, chief economist of UBS China, suggested that China's total GDP would surpass that
of the US either in 2016 or 2018. Her estimate assumes that China and the
US maintain their current rates of growth and the RMB will appreciate 5%
against the US dollar annually; China's GDP will then surpass that of the
US by 2016 and double it by 2021. Wang Jian, a Chinese economist,
pointed out that China's net industrial output surpassed that of the US for
the first time in 2009, and its industrial added value also surpassed that of
the US. Historically, the US surpassed Britain in industrial scale in 1892
and 20 years later, the US surpassed Britain in all aspects. He predicted that
the Chinese stock market would be four times that of the US in 2020.

Even based on the official exchange rate, most Western scholars today
seem to hold that the Chinese economy will surpass that of the US by
around 2030. Thus, it has become a mainstream view among economists
around the world that China will become the world's largest economy
within 10 to 20 years. Maddison also holds that it is very unprofessional
not to use the PPP method. I think that it is "seeking truth from facts" to
acknowledge China's backwardness in the past, but it is also "seeking truth
from facts" to acknowledge China's great progress since then. Like it or
not, China has risen, or to say the least China is now being held by many
as the "No. 2" in the world economy. Taking a longer-term view, China will
eventually be held as the "No. 1" in the future. One should of course
remain modest and prudent, and should not be carried away by whatever
successes or optimistic forecasts. China still faces many daunting challenges, and needs to be prepared for a rainy day. But one should also have
a long-term vision. If the size of the Chinese economy eventually surpasses

that of the US, how should China act on the world stage? How will it influence the world's future development, especially the evolution of the global economic and political order? Instead of being constantly self-deprecating as many are now, one should make preparations in advance. China needs a new big power awareness. A big power needs more wisdom, grander strategies and greater sense of responsibility; it should have its own rational discourse; it needs to reject big power chauvinism while endeavoring to make greater contributions to humanity.

CHAPTER 2

CHINA'S 1 + 1 > 2

2.1 The "Quasi-Developed Countries" within China

China is a large, populous and hugely complex country, and it is therefore not easy to understand China in average or per capita terms. This is comparable to a weather forecast for Singapore or China. If it is said that today's average temperature for Singapore is 32°C, people believe it, because Singapore is a small country with a total area about 1/25 of Beijing, but if it is announced that today's average temperature is 32°C for the People's Republic of China, it is simply meaningless to most people living in China, as the country is too vast and too complex in topography and climate conditions.

To assess China in average or per capita terms is similar to assessing China's climate in terms of its average temperature. To my mind, it would make much better sense if one could apply the idea of (1) *regional groups* and (2) *their interactions* as a way to understand this huge and complex country. Today's China is made up essentially of two regional groups, the first being the "quasi-developed countries" or the "developed region" and the other the "emerging economies" or the "emerging region", and the two groups are engaged in highly dynamic and mutually complementary interactions. And this is a main reason for China's rapid rise over the past three decades.

In April 2009, China's largest Internet portal Sina published an interesting article about some British university students' stay in Shanghai and their impression of China's developed region:

> Over 200 students from 35 British universities spent two weeks in Shanghai to experience the everyday life of the people here. As soon as

they set foot in Pudong Airport, they found that the airport was much bigger, more beautiful and modern than Heathrow, and Pudong Airport could be described as luxurious compared with Heathrow. When the students came to Nanjing Road, Shanghai's major shopping avenue, they found that it was ten times bigger than Oxford Street in London, and Shanghai's prosperity startled many of them, as in the British textbooks China is still often described as a very backward country.

Some students living with families of local residents were amazed by the kind of hi-fi electronic products in Chinese households, and some were surprised by the free TV coverage of English Premier League football matches. They found that in a typical Chinese family, over 120 TV channels could be received, compared with six or seven channels back in the UK. "This is perhaps the reason that Brits like to stay out in pubs," one student quipped. Some students were strongly interested in karaoke while others envied the richness and diversity of food available in people's daily lives.

At Pudong's Century Park, Hongqiao's Transport Hub, Xintiandi or Chenghuang Temple, at the sites of the World Expo, there were so many architectural wonders that they had never seen in their lifetime. At the top of the Shanghai World Financial Center and the Shanghai Stock Exchange, Chinese guides found that the students had become speechless. The cleanliness and efficiency of the Shanghai metro system, which seemed to be from a different generation compared to London's Tube; Shanghai's innovation zones; the science city of Zhangjiang; and numerous modern residential areas made the students unwilling to move their feet as they always wished to look a little more and take a few more pictures. Later they told their Chinese guides at the dinner table that China was more like a developed country.[1]

I have visited all the developed countries except Iceland and visited the UK many times, and I can understand the kind of shock felt by these British students for two reasons: first, the developed part of China is indeed changing fast and has become "more advanced" in many areas than

---

[1] http://blog.sina.com.cn/s/blog_4845eea90100d0xa.html, April 28, 2010.

the developed countries, and second, the Western media's biased coverage of China has created considerable misperceptions of China in the West. I well remember once on a flight from Berlin to Beijing, I sat next to two German ladies who were visiting China for the first time. They constantly asked me during the flight if they could get a taxi in Beijing, if it was easy to find a hotel in the city and if foreign currency exchange was available at the airport, but as soon as they set foot in the new terminal of Beijing International Airport, they were stunned by what they saw: the world's most modern and spectacular airport. I think they had never seen this kind of airport before, and the same is true with most foreigners. In fact, Berlin's airports are very modest, and can hardly match most airports in China's provincial capitals. It is reported that a new airport has been under construction in Berlin since 14 years ago with a total investment of US$3.4 billion, but it is not yet finished due to budget deficits and all kinds of lawsuits.

In all fairness, with three decades of reform, the gap between many parts of China and the developed countries is narrowing quickly, and the developed countries have been a bit too complacent for too many years, believing that they represent the best of everything in the world, and history has come to an end with the Western political and economic model. Yet China is actually catching up fast, and in this process, and to a certain extent, China is redefining what constitutes modernization.

Virtually all large and medium-sized cities in China are going through a facelift, and the kind of enthusiasm for modernization in China is what most Westerners have never seen in their lifetime, and is in many ways unprecedented in human history. Skyscrapers, highways, high-speed trains, shopping malls, urban metro systems and electric cars were all once products exclusive to the West, but today the West finds that in all these areas China leads the world, and often does them better, i.e. faster, newer, more stylish and more environment-friendly. No wonder when the *Daily Mail* of the UK reported the completion of the world's fastest high-speed train between Guangzhou and Wuhan within four years, many Internet users expressed their disbelief. One person observed, "Let's invite the Chinese engineers to Edinburgh where the construction of a railway of 12 miles with the highest speed of 70 kilometer/hour has lasted for three years, and will not be completed till 2011." An American commented,

"What a contrast with the World Trade Center here: eight years have passed, yet the site remains a hole." Another person wrote, "Look at Boston's projects, those greedy unions have caused 30% more spending and the project will not be completed in 20 years." Another person wrote, "Look at China, what a country can accomplish if one works single-mindedly? China is doing a great job."[2]

Naturally, it is not sufficient to look only at China's spectacular cities. The gap between cities and rural areas in China is still larger than in all the developed countries, and within cities, there are also issues of imbalances in development. It will be a long-term challenge for China to narrow such a gap, given the scale of the country and the size of its population. Yet if we look at the issue from another perspective, does it not represent the greatest opportunity for development in the world? According to a UN estimate, China experienced the world's most rapid urbanization over the past three decades, and it is my estimate that in the next two to three decades, China will continue to experience the world's fastest pace of urbanization, which will generate more opportunities for development than any other country in the world.

It is true that the urban-rural gap in China is quite large, but the Chinese rural areas have also undergone an enormous transformation over the past three decades, though smaller in scale than the cities. Some in China are so discontent with the urban-rural gap that they claim that our cities are like Europe and our countryside like Africa, which is grossly inaccurate.

Europe does not have the kind of dynamism shown abundantly in all Chinese cities, and many European cities such as Marseille, Rome and Naples are visibly behind China's first-tier cities, while most African cities, from my observation, have not yet reached the average level of the Chinese countryside. Africa's average life span is around 50, while in the Chinese countryside, it is around 70; in China's rural areas, color TV is widely available, and most people live in brick-built houses, while in Africa, many cities are still 50% made up of slums without power supply or running water, and most peasants live in huts, often without windows. According to the latest statistics of the United Nations, in sub-Saharan

---

[2] Quoted in *Qingnian Cankao* (Youth References), January 2010.

Africa, 89% of the rural people (i.e., 9 out of 10) has no access to electricity. And in developing countries, 41% of the rural population has no access to power supply. In contrast, 82% of the population in Tibet, China's least developed and most mountainous region, has access to electricity. This figure is higher than that in India, and is expected to reach 95% by 2015. China's plan to build highways to link all Chinese villages is about to be completed soon, something unimaginable for most developing countries.

One should also consider the potential value of the land in the Chinese countryside. China's land prices have gone up sharply over the past decades, and various experiments in land use are being carried out in China, which may well create immense wealth for China's rural population in the future. Yet it remains true that China still has a long way to go before its rural areas can all reach the level of the developed countries, and this process may well continue till China's urbanization process is complete.

China is simply too vast, populous and complex to be deciphered or understood easily. To avoid the trap of the "average temperature" approach mentioned earlier, it is advisable to understand China as a country made up of at least two groups of regions (further breakdowns are possible if need be) and to know (1) the characteristics of the two regional groups and (2) their interactions with each other. This will go a long way to help us better understand and explain China. The two groups can be described as follows.

The first group is what I call the "quasi-developed countries", while the other is the "emerging economies", and there are dynamic and mutually complementary interactions between them, which largely explain why China can rise so fast and how the future trajectory of China will evolve. Of course, what I have outlined is only a conceptual framework, and its more detailed elaboration will require the joint efforts of more social scientists.

Some general features of the two groups are already evident. The group of "quasi-developed countries" includes the coastal areas of China, particularly the Yangtze River Delta, the Pearl River Delta, the Beijing-Tianjin area, Liaoning Peninsula and Shandong Peninsula, as well as some inland cities. This is a vast region with a population of at least 300 million, or the size of the US population, and it has led the Chinese economic and social development and acquired all the major features of the developed countries: the people's average life span is between 75 and 82 years old, and the average life span in Beijing and Shanghai is higher than in New York; its overall infrastructure is better than that in the developed countries and it is also commercially more prosperous than most developed countries; its per capita GDP, if calculated in PPP, is between US$15,000 and US$25,000; its level of education is similar to that in most developed countries; its overall scientific and technological power is stronger than that of the average developed country; its home ownership is higher than that in the developed countries; the housing conditions for urban dwellers are better than those of Japan and Hong Kong. My field visits have also convinced me that most cities in this region have reached the level of southern Europe, notably Greece, Portugal, Spain and Italy, and its major metropolises are apparently more advanced than such cities as Rome, Athens, Lisbon, Marseille, Genoa and Naples. I retain the qualifier "quasi", because this regional group still behind developed countries in certain areas such as environmental standards and level of public civility. This is why China's developed region should still draw on others' strengths and strive to do better in the future.

According to the estimate of Angus Maddison in March 2009, the economic gap between China and the United States narrowed from 4.4 times in 1978 to 1.17 times in 2006. Considering the fact that the urban-rural gap in China is bigger than that in the United States, the gap between Chinese and American cities should be smaller than 1.17 times. This is perhaps why many Chinese from China's first-tier metropolises visiting New York ask the same question Thomas Friedman asked: who is living in the third world country?

A recent report released by the China Academy of Social Sciences on the competitiveness of Chinese provinces also confirms my observation: in 2008, Guangdong's GDP surpassed that of Saudi Arabia, Argentina and South Africa, and could rank No. 16 in the G20; the GDP of Shanghai, Beijing or Tianjin was already larger than that of some G20 countries, and Shanghai could rank No. 12 in the G20; and the economy of the Yangtze River Delta (Shanghai, Jiangsu and Zhejiang) was larger than that of South Korea or India. In fact, these estimates are still compiled on the basis of the official exchange rate, and if the PPP method is applied, the ranking will be more favorable to the Chinese provinces.[3]

2.2 The Size of China's Middle Class

With such a large group of "quasi-developed countries" within China, the country must have a large middle class. A report on this topic released by the Chinese Academy of Social Sciences confirms that China has entered a "golden age" in the growth of its middle class, which has reached 23% of the total population, i.e., about 300 million people, and is still expanding at 1% per year.[4] It is generally held that 40% of the population in Beijing and Shanghai should be considered as middle-class.

There is no universally agreed definition of what constitutes a "middle class". For instance, I myself have doubts about India's claim that it has 300 million middle-class people, as the impression I have gained from my several field visits to India is that India's middle class is far smaller than China's (perhaps one third or even less). I once consulted a senior Indian economist about how India arrived at its estimate of the size of its middle class. He told me that India used the estimate made by a World Bank economist named Martin Ravallion. I checked the criterion adopted by Ravallion and found that his criterion was quite broad; basically, anyone with a daily income of US$2 to US$13 (calculated on PPP basis) would be considered as middle-class, and he argued that once a person's daily income reached US$2, that person was out of abject poverty. I also checked his conclusion on China and India when the same criterion was applied, and his conclusion was that by the year 2005, China's middle class was 800 million while India's was 264 million.[5] Ravallion's criterion is a bit too low by Chinese standards, as most Chinese are unlikely to accept the claim

---

[3] Li Jianping, Li Mingrong, Gao Yanjing (eds.), *Annual Report on Overall Competitiveness of China's Provincial Economy 2008–2009*, Social Sciences Academic Press, Beijing, 2010.
[4] See the interview with Prof. Lu Xueyi, *Zhongguo Qingnianbao* (China Youth Daily), February 11, 2010.
[5] See the Special Report on the New Middle Classes in Emerging Markets, *The Economist*, February 12, 2009.

that there are 800 million middle-class people in China, but his study does confirm my estimate that India's middle class is much smaller than China's.

The Asian Development Bank (ADB) issued a report in 2010 which claims that China's middle class has reached 817 million, and its criterion is similar to that used by Ravallion, i.e., a daily income between US$2 and US$20. The ADB further divides the Chinese middle class into three categories — lower middle class, middle middle class and upper middle class — and concludes that there are 303 million Chinese belonging to the lower middle class, with the rest belonging to the middle middle or upper middle class. Yet somehow the Chinese always prefer a higher bar for themselves, and in China today, only a minority of the people acknowledge their middle-class status. In India, when you ask a hotel porter if he belongs to the middle class, he will say yes, although he may live in a slum, but in Beijing or Shanghai, if you ask those young office workers sipping coffee in Starbucks if they are middle-class, their likely reply is "No, as I've got only one apartment, not two."

In fact, the largest fortune for most people in the developed countries is perhaps one property, either an apartment or a house. I tend to think that if one defines middle-class status only with economic criteria, perhaps a stable job plus a property or something equivalent would suffice, and this is by no means low criteria, nor is it designed exclusively for China, as home ownership is about 60% in countries like France, Japan and the United States, largely reflecting the size of the middle class in those countries. Some Chinese have coined the term "housing slaves", referring to those burdened with housing loans and interest payments. But this is true everywhere, including the developed countries, where few choose to pay back housing loans before the age of 55. In fact, a bank's offer of a housing loan to you in most countries means its recognition of your middle-class status.

China's home ownership is already higher than that of most developed countries, and this is undoubtedly a great achievement of China over the past decades. If my economic criteria hold, China's middle class should be larger than Japan's total population (130 million), and it is perhaps somewhere between four times the population of France (260 million) and the US population (300 million) or slightly larger than the US population.

Some consumer spending statistics may help us size up China's middle class. As early as 2003, China's outbound tourists reached 20.2 million trips a year, surpassing Japan for the first time; the average Chinese tourists have spent more in France than their Japanese counterparts since 2009; China has become the largest producer and consumer of automobiles since 2009, indicating that there has emerged dozens of millions of automobile consumers; by the end of 2009, Chinese spending on luxury goods surpassed American spending, ranking second in the world, or making up roughly 25% of the world's total. In 2010 almost one third of Swiss watches were exported to the Chinese mainland and Hong Kong, where the largest group of customers are mainland tourists who flock to Hong Kong to buy tax-free watches. Value judgment on luxury consumption aside, these facts seem to suggest that the Chinese consumption power is not confined, as alleged by some critics, to a minority of the super-rich. On the contrary, a very large middle class has emerged in China.

One can even make a comparison with the US in terms of the aforementioned median household net worth, which is between US$84,000 and US$93,000 in the US, or between 535,000 and 593,000 *yuan* at the exchange rate of October 2011, and my own estimate is that perhaps there are already 100 million or so households in China with at least this level of household net worth. Naturally, the rising property prices in China account to a great extent for the rising net assets, and after all Japan's household net worth was once higher than that of the US during the period of its housing bubble. But we should also consider the fact that the Chinese currency is widely viewed as undervalued and the average size of the Chinese household is smaller than the American one.

A study conducted by Tsinghua University in 2008 confirms my estimate. Based on sample surveys of 2,100 households from 15 Chinese cities, the study reveals that the urban average household net worth in China is 600,700 *yuan* or about US$95,000, and of the total household assets, housing represents the largest share (62.72%), followed by cash and bank deposits (over 15%). This study is not about the "median" but the "average", and as far as I know, there is still no survey on the median household net worth in China, but this study already serves to highlight the fact that most of China's urban residents are no longer poor by international standards. Furthermore, this is a study conducted in 2008, and the assets of

Chinese urban households have been increasing since then. No nation has experienced faster wealth creation than China over the past three decades, and this fact alone should allow us to assess favorably the China model.

It is also necessary to point out that although the median household net worth in the United States is not very large, the United States remains the world's No. 1 consumer market for several reasons. First, the "median" statistics tend to skip the rich group. Take the year 2004 as an example. Over 7.5 million American households had a net worth of more than US$1 million, constituting a large consumption group. Furthermore, Americans have perhaps the strongest culture of credit consumption. In fact, the whole country of the US lives on credit, and it is therefore understandable that the United States has become the world's largest consumer market, but its excessive reliance on credit consumption is also the main cause of the current financial crisis. Furthermore, the US dollar is still the major international reserve currency, and other countries still buy US Treasury bonds, and the United States also uses its power to influence such countries like Japan to appreciate their currencies as a way to reduce American debt.

Aware of the nature of the problem, China is increasingly linking the Chinese RMB with a basket of currencies and striving to turn the RMB into a major international reserve currency in the future. While the United States may feel the pressure from China's effort, on the part of China, it is necessary to guard against a possible financial crisis triggered by Washington's irresponsible policies, as such a crisis could be disastrous for China and even set back the Chinese economy by decades and lead the country to political turmoil. Yet looking at the issue from another angle, the American culture of credit consumption is also relevant to China. One should not copy the American way of over-reliance on credit consumption, but some degree of credit consumption should be encouraged in China at least to make better use of the household assets held by so many Chinese families today. Indeed, in the United States, an individual without any credit is often viewed with suspicion, and in Switzerland, those who repay their housing loan are often viewed as the rich class subject to a higher level of fortune tax. China should not copy the credit consumption in the West, but a certain level of credit consumption would be positive for the Chinese economy, and for China's shift from an economy excessively relying on foreign trade to one relying more on domestic consumption.

2.3 The "Emerging Economies" within China

In addition to the aforementioned group of "quasi-developed countries" within China, the rest of China, its interior part in particular, may be described as the group of "emerging economies". "Emerging economies" has often been used to refer to those fast-growing countries or regions over the past decades. From my point of view, only this concept can capture the key features of this regional group in China, and these features include the following.

First, if a typical developing country is marked by a high rate of illiteracy, widespread poverty and a subsistence economy, this regional group in China has already moved beyond such a dismal level of development. This group has largely eradicated extreme poverty and achieved compulsory secondary education. Its people are industrious and intelligent, and while they are not yet very rich, they have their own land and housing, and with enough food and daily necessities, they are obviously better off than 50% of the people in any typical developing country.

Second, this group is dynamic and growing fast. In fact, China's interior has been growing faster than China's coastal areas over the past three years. Take the year 2009 as an example. The GDP of China's 13 interior provinces grew over 10% a year, and Inner Mongolia grew at 17% a year for seven years running, making it the fastest-growing province in China.

Third, the group has its own advantages, particularly in terms of human and natural resources, and it is engaged in extensive mutually beneficial exchanges with China's developed regions in the fields of human and natural resources, consumer goods and technology. Thanks to this kind of positive interaction between the two regional groups, these provinces themselves are becoming ever larger consumer markets and have attracted a lot of foreign and domestic investments.

Fourth, as the developed group moves up the value chain, more and more industries are being transferred from China's developed regions to the "emerging economies". In recent years, the state has upgraded several regional development strategies for China's interior regions to the level of national development strategies accompanied by more favorable policies for investors, and the interior part of China is now witnessing an accelerated pace of industrialization and urbanization.

Fifth, growth poles have also emerged within this group. Although weaker in development conditions than the developed group, this group has its comparative advantages in certain areas such as agriculture, equipment manufacturing, extractive industries and certain high-tech industries. It is also doing a better job than many coastal provinces in tapping China's interior market and promoting a more harmonious development between urban and rural areas. Chongqing is a good example in this regard. Its dynamic mayor Huang Qifan observed in March 2010:

> Chongqing's objective is to become, by the year 2020, the economic center and a major growth pole of the western part of China. Chongqing is known to have both large urban areas and large rural areas, and it will be turned into a metropolis of balanced development of urban and rural areas. Chongqing witnessed a high growth rate of 14.9% in 2009, ranking the third nationwide, and is expected to grow at 16% in 2010. Although located in the interior, Chongqing is proactive in attracting foreign direct investment. In 2007, its total FDI was only US$1 billion, but that was quadrupled by 2010 to become US$4 billion, and is expected to grow to US$6 billion by 2011.

Mayor Huang also noted:

> At this moment, 51% of the people in Chongqing live in urban areas while 49% in rural areas, but in the coming years, its urban population will increase to 70%. The future of Chongqing will be a cluster of three layers of cities: one metropolis, 30 medium cities, and 100 small cities. And to make it a success, Chongqing is carrying out a five-Chongqing program, namely, a livable Chongqing, a green Chongqing, a traffic-smooth Chongqing, a safe Chongqing, and a healthy Chongqing.

Chongqing seems well on its way to achieve these objectives. Beyond Chongqing, a national highway network has been completed, and a network of high-speed trains is expected to be completed in a decade or so, and all this goes a long way to promote the mutually beneficial interactions between the two regional groups in China. China already has the busiest circulation of people and goods in the world. China's old division of labor and production based on self-contained industries along provincial divisions is being replaced by a more rational division of labor and production across the nation, and a unified and efficient domestic market is fast emerging. With further interactions between the two groups, regional gaps will decline, a more balanced development will set in, and this process, I believe, will continue till China becomes the world's largest developed country.

2.4 Why China's 1 + 1 > 2?

The difficulty of understanding a huge and complex country like China is like in the famous fable of the blind men and the elephant, with the blind men all claiming that various parts of the elephant, whether the ears, long nose or huge body, represent the whole elephant. The official line most often heard about China is that while China is already the second-largest economy in terms of its overall GDP, it still ranks very low in terms of per capita GDP. Yet, this description fails to explain China clearly, as it does not distinguish between matters of quantity and quality. I am myself inclined to use the aforementioned idea of two regional groups and their interactions to explain China.

In fact, this approach helps to highlight the relationship between quantity and quality. If one simply discusses China at the level of overall GDP or per capita GDP, it is a matter of quantity, not quality. But the difference between developed and developing nations is less an issue of quantity, and more an issue of quality; it is the difference between pre-modern and modern states.

As stated earlier, today's China is made up of two regional groups, namely the developed one and the newly emerging one. If the former represents mainly a modern economy, modern management, modern R&D and modern services, then the latter can be said to represent the scale effect. The combination of the strengths of the two groups is tantamount to the combination of quality and quantity, thus producing the amazing effect of 1 + 1 > 2 and the fast rise of China.

According to Chinese economist Hu Angang, in 1993, the number of Internet users in the US was 3,000 times that in China, but in 2008, the number in China was 1.2 times that in the US; in 1987, the mobile phone population in the US was 1,760 times that in China, but now, it is only 40% of

China's. Most economists predicted that by 2020, China would become the world's largest automobile market, but in reality, it became so in 2009. The rise of China and its model of development have now become global hot topics, not due to China's deliberate plan, but due to the fact that the outside world is constantly experienced the 1 + 1 > 2 impact from China.

Second, the idea of regional groups helps us understand the real China. I have already mentioned how the "average temperature" approach fails to convince others about the real China. If one claims that China is a developing country, most people who know the real third world find it hard to accept, because in many domains, and in most parts of the rural areas, China is doing better than the developing countries. The same is true with only claiming China as the second-largest economy, as it tends to ignore the underdeveloped dimension of China. The essence of China today, I think, can be much better grasped if one understands the idea of the two regional groups and their interactive relations.

Some Swiss watch-making companies such as TAG Heuer were influenced by the "average temperature" approach and regarded China as a poor developing country. As a result they grossly underestimated the Chinese market and kept their eyes on the traditional US and Japanese markets, and so they suffered huge losses from the fallout of the financial crisis. However, some others such as Omega had a clear sense of China's regional groups and understood that the developed regions in China alone could represent a market larger than that of Japan or even the US, and these companies have enjoyed a boom in recent years. It is also not too much of an exaggeration to say that China's developed regions have to some extent saved the Swiss watch industry since 2008.

The idea of two regional groups is also important for us to assess more accurately our own domestic situation. We should not always use "China is still a developing country" as a pretext to excuse our own mistakes. China's first-tier cities like Beijing and Shanghai should compare themselves with cities like New York, London, Paris and Tokyo and take concrete steps to do well and even outperform these cities in more and more areas. China's developed regions should use the developed countries as their references in their work so as to eventually do better than those developed countries. Likewise, China's newly emerging regions should find their own references in the world and try to reach a new high.

Third, the idea of regional groups could turn our current static read-ing of China into a dynamic one. Indeed, China's rise is not a statistics game that can be altered at will. The 1 + 1 is not Europe + Africa, as Europe's relationship with Africa is, as many have argued, a continuation of a postcolonial relationship which hinders, rather than facilitates, Africa's development. For instance, Europe's huge agricultural subsidies do not allow Africa to develop its comparative advantages in agriculture. In con-trast, within China, the two regional groups are bound by blood ties, a shared language and cultural traditions, and their complementary and interactive partnership is secured and promoted by a neutral and efficient central government. This underpins the immense dynamism in the Chinese economy and society.

Fourth, the 1 + 1 > 2 formula has underlined China's strategic consid-erations and to a certain extent explained why Deng Xiaoping was so eager to press those regions with better initial conditions to move ahead first. Deng held that in the West-dominated world, China might remain forever in a state of passivity vulnerable to bullying by the Western powers if China did not have its own developed regions, and China might well become an immediate victim if there were a major international financial or other crisis. The tragedy of the 1997 Asian financial crisis and its impact on countries like Thailand and Indonesia and the impact of the 2008 financial crisis on Eastern Europe all serve to illustrate this point. Deng repeatedly stated that "China should build several Hong Kongs" and "Shanghai is China's trump card", knowing that the rise of a vast devel-oped region within China would also mean the emergence of China's own competitive industries, multinationals, brand names as well as a large consumer population.

This reminds me of the famous Chinese story about Tian Ji's horse racing in 4th Century BC. The story goes like this: General Tian Ji of the Qi state was perplexed by his constant failures in horse racing, and Sun Bin, a great military strategist and descendant of Sun Tzu, the author of the famous *Art of War*, counseled him to rearrange his horses in such a way that his best horse would compete with the second-best horse of his oppo-nent, his second-best horse would compete with his opponent's worst horse, and his worst horse would compete with his opponent's best horse, and eventually General Tian Ji won the race two to one. The philosophy of the story is to make best use of one's relative and asymmetrical strength in any competition with one's more powerful competitors.

In a world order dominated by the West, China is on the whole a weaker player, but with a strategy to ensure the fast rise of a huge developed region, China has created its relative and asymmetrical strength. When Thomas Friedman noted that Shanghai, Beijing and Dalian were doing better than New York in many aspects, he in a way acknowledged the impact of China's relative and asymmetrical strength versus that of the United States. With this approach, China's chance of winning the international competition is significantly enhanced. China's competitiveness in such fields as the space industry, ship-building, electronics, high-speed trains, automobiles and urban metro systems are all inseparable from this spatial distribution of China's economic and technological power.

In many ways, the developed countries themselves are also striving to shape a 1 + 1 > 2 scenario, as shown by the expansion of the European Union into the relatively poor Eastern Europe and the establishment of the North American Free Trade Area (NAFTA) which includes the poor but populous Mexico. Indeed, the developed world finds itself in a situation of saturated demand and increased labor costs, and therefore needs developing partners, but up to now, neither the EU nor the NAFTA has produced a 1 + 1 > 2 effect as desired, especially compared with China's success in this regard. China's 1 + 1 > 2 effect is a product of the Chinese civilizational state, which I will elaborate on in the next chapter, while Europe and the United States face greater challenges when they want to integrate with other countries beyond their civilizational boundaries.

In discussing China's internal issues, we also need a sense of the regional groups and their interrelations. Some people have a tendency to negate China's successes by focusing on China's problems. There are many problems in this fast-growing and changing country, but China's population is four times that of the United States, and it is not at all strange if China faces four times more problems than the United States. Given the scale of the country and the size of its population, we need to look at China with an awareness of its size, complexity and diversity. For instance, in tackling corruption or ensuring good governance, one may compare China's developed regions with the developed countries, and from my point of view, it is safe to say that corruption in Shanghai is much lower than in Italy, and Shanghai is in many ways a better-governed city than New York, and the Yangtze River Delta (Shanghai, Jiangsu and Zhejiang) is better governed than Greece or Italy. This is by no means a small achievement, as in terms of population, Shanghai is the size of two Greeces or three Switzerlands; Jiangsu province seven Greeces or ten Belgiums; and China's developed regions are roughly the size of 20 average European countries. Any success in so vast and populous a region will have a demonstrative effect on the whole country and beyond. If the developed part of China can outperform the developed countries in various areas, other parts of China may eventually catch up, and in fact some are already catching up fast, like Inner Mongolia and Chongqing, the largest interior metropolis with 30 million people. After all, the China model is always marked by both competition and cooperation between different regions.

Last but not least, the 1 + 1 > 2 effect has produced what can be called the 20/80 effect or the famous law of the vital few, a concept invented by Italian economist Vilfredo Pareto, which argues that roughly 80% of the effects in everything come from 20% of the causes. In business it is a rule of thumb, i.e., 80% of one's sales usually come from 20% of one's clients. In China today, the developed regions or 20% of the country create 80% of the nation's wealth. Within the newly emerging regions, the same rule applies, as 20% of the areas within the regions such as Chongqing, Chengdu and Xi'an are creating 80% of the wealth in interior China. This pattern of the 20/80 effect will continuously expand till the whole country is modernized.

This dynamic approach to development, however, carries with it certain risks, as it implies that regional gaps may actually expand rather than narrow during a certain period of time, but we should have a historical and long-term vision for China's development. With the exception of very small countries, no country can achieve simultaneous development across the country. In the case of the United States, its east coast developed first, then the west; in France, Paris first, then the rest of France; in Japan, the Kyoto and Tokyo regions before other regions. In other words, wealth accumulation in certain regions gradually spread to the rest of the country.

In my book *Zhongguo Chudong Quanqiu* (China Touches the World), I cited the Pudong district of Shanghai as an example to show the importance of building a mutually complementary mechanism between the developed regions and the less developed regions in China. For instance, the Pudong district is much richer than China's Guizhou province, but 51.4% of Pudong's revenue goes to the central government, which in turn goes to help other parts of China, including Guizhou. If such a mechanism is established between the rich and poor regions of China, one does not need to be over-concerned about the regional gaps, as this is like having one member of a family who is good at creating wealth but also ready to help other members of the family, thus shaping a benign cycle positive for the future of the whole family.[6]

China's developed regions are like Pudong, and their strength is in concentrating more human talents and financial resources, and then making an impact on the whole country. This understanding has come the hard way, as the country experienced for a long time the negative effect of excessive egalitarianism which led to China's overall egalitarianism and overall poverty. Indeed, international experience seems to suggest that it is by no means easy to narrow regional gaps for a large and diverse country, and the best way to narrow such a gap is to establish mechanisms linking the rich and poor regions. Deng Xiaoping's observations such as "China should build several Hong Kongs", "Shanghai is our trump card" and "Guangdong should take the lead in surpassing the 'four little dragons'" all serve to illustrate his long-term strategies for China's development. He encouraged some parts of China to get rich first so as to bring the rest of the country to prosperity. It is heartening that Deng's vision has come to fruition in China today.

---

[6] Zhang Weiwei, *Zhongguo Chudong Quanqiu* (China Touches the World), Xinhua Press, Beijing, 2008, pp. 124–125.

CHAPTER 3

THE RISE OF A CIVILIZATIONAL STATE

3.1 China's Rocky Path towards a Nation-State

What is the nature of China's rise? This is a question on which China's future hinges. One view in China holds that China's rise is none other than that of an ordinary country that has carried out reforms in accordance with the Western theory of the market economy and thus enjoyed rapid development, and with a growing middle class, the country will accept more and more Western ideas and institutional arrangements and eventually become part of the Western world. Another view holds that China's rise represents the rise of a different type of country, and the major reason for China's rise is its adherence to its own path of development, and the country has thus, on the one hand, learnt a lot from other countries and, on the other hand, given play to its own strengths and moved beyond the Western model, and it is the rise of a *civilizational state* which has amalgamated the world's longest continuous civilization with a huge modern state. I take the latter view.

Some people think that the Western model represents the supreme ideal of mankind, and all China should do is to make an economic, social and political transition to the Western model. But to my mind, if a civilizational state like China follows the Western model, the country will experience chaos and break up. Indeed, in retrospect, if China had followed the Western model rather than adhering to its own path, the country could have disintegrated just like the Soviet Union and Yugoslavia.

China's rise is due to its own model of development which the West does not endorse, but China is likely to continue to move along its own chosen path and become the world's largest economy with all its impact on the world at large. Yet this does not mean that China and the West will be necessarily moving on a collision course. On the contrary, the nature of China as a civilizational state determines that given its cultural traditions, China is not likely to be a country bent on confrontation. Rather, it is more likely to seek peaceful co-existence, mutual learning and win-win outcomes with other countries and other political systems, and this is indeed good for the rest of the world. But this positive picture may change if some countries are determined to pick a fight with China.

In order to understand the rise of a civilizational state, it is perhaps useful to recall our understanding of the concept of a nation-state. A nation-state generally refers to a state made up of people who share some common traits such as language, religion and way of life. Europe is the birthplace of nation-states, and nationalism propelled much of Europe's nationhood and modernization. But nationalism proved a major cause of conflicts and wars in Europe and beyond. During the 18th and 19th centuries, nation-states emerged one after another in Europe.

The earliest nation-state in Europe is arguably France. The French emperors unified taxation and armies of various vassal states in the late 18th century and early 19th century, shaped a strong mobilization power and defeated on many occasions the various Prussian states. But when "blood and iron" Chancellor Bismarck unified Germany into a nation-state in 1871, Germany rose fast and embarked on a path of military expansionism.

In Asia, Japan went through the Meiji Restoration and became a nation-state, and defeated China in 1895, which was then not yet a nation-state. At that time, China's GDP was larger than both that of Britain and Japan, but two countries had already become nation-states with the kind of power for national unity and war mobilization that China lacked. Triggered by the repeated military failures, China embarked on its own path of building a nation-state from the early 20th century onwards. In the Western political discourse, a nation-state is almost synonymous with a modern state, and vice versa. The two concepts are by no means perfect, but I will employ them here for the sake of convenience.

Back in the 19th and 20th centuries, China was still a traditional agricultural society with 95% of its population living off the land. At that time, the Chinese countryside was essentially a kinship society, often with one village made up of people with the same surname, and the well-educated country gentry could handle independently most village affairs, especially matters between villages or between kinships. On the surface, the Chinese emperor had a lot of power over the country, yet as a saying goes, "The sky is high, and the emperor is far away": the central government was nominally powerful, but weak in reality, and to a great extent, it did not have enough technical means to govern the country, and thus relied heavily on moral and ideological education. The central government did not have the kind of organizational or mobilization power as the Western nation-states, and Beijing even did not have many troops under its control. By the mid-19th century, China's traditional state was no longer able to cope with the challenges posed by Western nation-states or modern states, as shown by the fact that China lost the First Opium War to the British in 1840, the Second Opium War to both the British and the French in 1860 and then the Sino-Japanese War to the Japanese in 1895.

Some Western scholars have already used the concept of a civilization-state to describe China, arguing that while China's nation-state was still in the process of formation, China as a civilization-state had a history of several thousands of years. The Chinese nation lived on its soil and evolved its own unique civilization, and its rather comprehensive form of a state could at least be traced to Emperor Qin Shihuang's first unification of China in 221 BC. But the concept of a "civilization-state" was applied to mean that China was still faced with many difficulties when it was trying to make the transition from a civilization-state to a nation-state, and they blamed China's thousands of years of civilization for being a burden on its effort to build a modern state. In other words, being a civilization-state, China found it hard to evolve modern laws, economics, defense, education and political governance. Joseph R. Levenson, a Harvard scholar, presented this view in his book *Confucian China and Its Modern Fate*. Most Western scholars held the view that throughout the 20th century, China's history was basically a process of transition from a civilization-state to a nation-state, from the idea of "heaven" to the idea of a "state". Lucian Pye, another American political scientist, even described China as "a civilization pretending to be a nation-state".[1]

Nevertheless, unremitting efforts were being made to turn China into a modern nation-state, and China did it the hard way. The efforts started with the Republican Revolution of 1911, which put an end to the last dynasty, the Qing Dynasty, continued with the May 4th movement of 1919 through the period of warlords in the 1920s, and the victory of the Northern Expedition of 1926–1927 and the War of Resistance against Japanese Aggression (1937–1945) till the founding of the People's Republic. At the cost of tens of millions of lives, the Chinese have finally established a nation-state in the modern sense, and since then, with more efforts at nation-building, at reform and opening up, China is now the world's second-largest economy and well on its way to becoming the largest in the coming decade.

The late historian Ray Huang (Huang Renyu) made a pertinent argument which I share. He summarized the contemporary history of China from what he called "a macro historical perspective". He treated the Republican period (1911–1949) as a whole and held that the Kuomintang regime during this period succeeded in reshaping an upper structure for the modern state of China, which included various government ministries, the central bank, and the modern educational system, but this upper structure was out of touch with the grassroots of the Chinese society. Huang argued that Mao's communist revolution since the 1920s based on land reforms and mobilization of the peasants in turn reshaped a lower structure for the Chinese state. Indeed, Mao's efforts to organize peasant associations at the grassroots level and his land reform and literacy campaigns all paved the way for the so-called "numerical management" or modern economic management of China at a later stage. Huang argued further that Deng's economic reform and opening up since 1979 reshaped a middle structure commensurate with a modern market economy, ranging from a modern taxation system to a comprehensive judicial system to millions of banking branches to nationwide logistics for

---

[1] Lucian Pye, "Social Science Theories in Search of Chinese Realities", *China Quarterly*, 132 (1992), p. 1162.

material goods.[2] With the three structures in place, China's status as a modern nation-state is established. However, some people in China still believe that unless China adopts the Western political system, China will not be a modern state. But this is a marginalized view with little support in China.

3.2 The Rise of a Civilizational State

Today's China, with the aforementioned three structures, has established an unprecedented modern state system which includes a unified government, market, economy, education, law, defense, finance and taxation, and the Chinese state is among the most competent ones in the world, as shown by its organization of the Olympic Games in 2008 and its guidance for the country's economic growth. Yet it still retains its many traditions associated with a civilization-state, and these traditions are playing a vital role today in the world's most populous nation.

British scholar and writer Martin Jacques published in 2009 an influential yet controversial book titled *When China Rules the World*.[3] Although the title of the book does not fit into the Chinese way of thinking or behaving, Jacques has gone significantly beyond the Euro-centric view of a civilization-state and given the concept a more positive assessment. One of his major arguments is as follows:

> There are many civilizations — Western civilization is one example — but China is the only civilization-state. It is defined by its extraordinarily long history and also its huge geographic and demographic scale and diversity. The implications are profound: Unity is its first priority, plurality the condition of its existence (which is why China could offer Hong Kong "one country two systems," a formula alien to a nation-state).

---

[2] Rey Huang (Huang Renyu), 《中国大历史》 (China: A Macro History), Lianjing Press, Taipei, 1993.

[3] Martin Jacques, *When China Rules the World: The End of the Western World and the Birth of a New Global Order*, Penguin, New York, 2009.

The Chinese state enjoys a very different kind of relationship with society compared with the Western state. It enjoys much greater natural authority, legitimacy and respect, even though not a single vote is cast for the government. The reason is that the state is seen by the Chinese as the guardian, custodian and embodiment of their civilization. The duty of the state is to protect its unity. The legitimacy of the state therefore lies deep in Chinese history. This is utterly different from how the state is seen in Western societies.[4]

He cites my view on the China model in his book and holds that this model will become attractive to other countries. His observations on China as a civilization-state are helpful for better understanding the rise of China and its relations with the West and his views have also inspired some of my research on China as a civilizational state.

Yet, interestingly, despite his break with Euro-centric perceptions, Jacques still perceives a tension between the nation-state and the civilization-state, and this tension may, he argues, lead China in different directions. For instance, he hypothesizes that China may eventually revive a certain form of the ancient tributary system, characteristic of China's past relations with its supposedly inferior neighbors, and the alleged Chinese sense of racial superiority may pose a challenge to the existing international order.[5] From this perspective, Jacques does not yet seem to be totally free from the core belief of many Western scholars that there is an inherent mismatch between nation-state and civilization-state.

For me, however, today's China is already a civilizational state, which amalgamates the nation-state and the civilization-state, and combines the strength of both. This fact itself is a miracle, highlighting the Chinese civilization's known capacity and tradition for creating synergies.

As a modern state, China accepts the concept of the sovereign equality of states and prevailing conceptions of human rights. China is not likely to

---

[4] *Los Angeles Times,* November 22, 2009.

[5] For Martin Jacques's views on the tributary system and the race issue, see pp. 374–376 on "the return of the tributary system" and pp. 380–382 on "the Chinese racial order" in Martin Jacques, *When China Rules the World: The End of the Western World and the Birth of a New Global Order,* Penguin, New York, 2009.

restore the tributary system, nor will China embrace racism. China is first of all a modern state, but unique due to the many traditions and features originating from its civilization. This is also the key conceptual difference between a civilizational state and a civilization-state. The former represents an amalgamation of an old civilization and a modern nation-state, while the latter often reflects the tension between the two.

As a civilizational state, China is both old and young, both traditional and modern, both Chinese and international. At least eight features can be distilled from the civilizational state of China, and these features are (1) a super-large population, (2) a super-vast territory, (3) super-long traditions, (4) a super-rich culture, (5) a unique language, (6) unique politics, (7) a unique society and (8) a unique economy, or simply the "four supers" and "four uniques", each of which combines the elements of the old Chinese civilization and the new modern state.

(1) *Super-large Population*

One fifth of the world's population lives in China. The average size of a European country is about 14 million people, and China is approximately the size of 100 average European countries. A civilizational state is a product of "hundreds of states amalgamated into one" over China's long and continuous history. India's population is also large and second only to China's, but India was not a unified state until the British rule in the second half of the 19th century, as compared with China's first unification back in 221 BC. As a result, the Indian population is far less homogeneous than the Chinese. In China 92% of the Chinese identify themselves as Han Chinese.

The Western countries as a whole represent only 14% of the world's population, while China 19%. With the establishment of a modern state, especially a modern educational system, China's educated population is China's greatest asset. With both modern education and traditional cultural values, China's large population has produced an impact on a scale unprecedented in human history, and a feature of the China model can be summarized as follows: China's capacity for learning, adaptation and innovation, together with an unmatched scale effect thanks to the size of the population, has produced immense internal and external impacts.

China's rapid progress in such areas as tourism, automobile industry, the Internet, high-speed trains and urbanization has demonstrated this scale effect. Investors in China tend to share one belief: if they can achieve the No. 1 status in China, they may well be the No. 1 in the world.

In a broad sense, it is perhaps not far-fetched to claim that due to the size of the population, China may change the world so long as it changes itself. For instance, China has become the world's largest producer and consumer of automobiles, so all global automobile firms are now in China, and the world automobile industry has started some kind of China-oriented transition. Likewise, China now is engaged in the world's largest urbanization programs, and the world's best architectural firms are competing with each other for the Chinese market and have started some kind of China-oriented transition. This trend is likely to continue in ever more areas such as tourism, air transport, the movie industry, sports, education, alternative energies and even models of development and political governance.

(2) *Super-vast Territory*

China is a continent, and its vast territory has taken shape over its long history with a gradual amalgamation of "hundreds of states". Russia and Canada are larger than China in terms of territory, but they have never experienced the kind of integration process as a civilizational state. The Soviet Union tried to create the Soviet nation in the vast territory of the USSR but failed with the collapse of the country, while Canada has a small population and short history.

Some people admire the many advantages of small countries, which is understandable. But all countries have their own advantages and disadvantages, and small countries are often more vulnerable to various shocks than big ones. A senior Singaporean diplomat based in Geneva once told me that "Singapore is indeed a prosperous country, but it is extremely careful in managing state affairs, as any careless mistake could be costly. For instance, if a 9/11-type terrorist attack occurred in Singapore, it could spell the end of my country." Chile is a relatively prosperous developing country, but the 2010 earthquake hit the country hard and caused its GDP to drop. In comparison, for a large country like China, the huge 2008 earthquake of Sichuan did not affect the country's overall economy.

Its vast territory gives China certain geopolitical and geoeconomic advantages that few other countries have. China has established a strong state and a powerful defense capability, and gone are the days when foreign powers could bully and invade China at will, as was the case in China's century of humiliations from the mid-19th to the mid-20th century. It also allows China to carry out large-scale projects, rare in human history, such as the supply of natural gas from the western to eastern regions, and nationwide highway and high-speed train networks. For most countries, any move up in the value chain often means that labor-intensive industries will be out-sourced, but in China's vast territory, most of these industries gain a new lease on life as they are transferred to other parts of China. In China's modernization process, local and central governments both play an important role, which Chairman Mao used to call "walking on two legs", and this is also determined by the sheer size of the country and its population.

Being a civilizational state provides China with a unique geo-strategic "radiation". Over the past three decades, China has pursued an open-door policy along China's border regions, and signed a free trade agreement with ASEAN countries, established the Shanghai Cooperation Organization with Russia and Central Asian republics and promoted economic integration with Japan and South Korea, and with other entities of Greater China (Hong Kong, Macau and Taiwan). In effect, China has become the locomotive for the regional economic growth and for the world's economic recovery, and this is inseparable from China's geo-strategic location in the heart of East Asia, the world's most dynamic region of development.

(3) *Super-long Traditions*

Being the world's longest continuous civilization has allowed China's traditions to evolve, develop and adapt in virtually all branches of human knowledge and practices, such as political governance, economics, education, art, music, literature, architecture, military, sports, food and medicine. The original, continuous and endogenous nature of these traditions is indeed rare and unique in the world.

China draws on its ancient traditions and wisdoms. In the field of political governance, several key concepts used in today's political governance all originate from the ancient times. For instance, today's concept of "keeping pace with the changing times" (*yushi jujin*) is derived from the idea of *yushi xiexin* (keeping up with the times) contained in the *I Ching* or the *Book of Changes*, dating back to China's Warring States period (mid-4th to early 3rd century BC), and the same is true of today's concept of "building a harmonious society", which originates from the ancient concept of *taihe* (overall harmony) contained in the same classic. Deng Xiaoping's idea of "crossing the river by feeling for stepping stones", which has guided China's reform and opening up, is in fact a popular proverb from the ancient times. And the historical roots of these ideas have apparently given them added legitimacy and facilitated their general acceptance by the people.

The China model and the Chinese political narratives also reflect the independent and endogenous nature of the Chinese civilization. In a way it is similar to Chinese traditional medicine: whether Western medicine can explain it or not, most Chinese have trust in its efficacy, and if Western medicine cannot explain such efficacy, just as Western social sciences still fail to predict or explain the success of the China model, this is not a problem of whether Chinese medicine or the China model is scientific or not. Rather, it highlights more the limitations of Western medicine or social sciences originating in the West, which have yet to develop further to explain the effects of Chinese medicine or the China model. What Chinese social scientists should do is not "cut one's feet to suit Western shoes"; rather they should base themselves on the successful Chinese experience and rethink many preconceived ideas originating from the Western experience, and revise, if need be, the Western textbooks or create China's own theories.

It has also been proved that an appropriate combination of Chinese medicine and Western medicine tends to produce a better overall effect. This analogy applies to the China model, as it has already drawn a lot on the Western ideas and practices, but has managed to keep its own essence, thus producing far better overall results than the Western model.

(4) *Super-rich Culture*

With its long and continuous history, China has developed one of the richest cultural heritages in the world, and Chinese culture is in fact the synergy of the cultures of "hundreds of states" over China's long history. Chinese culture stresses the holistic unity of heaven and earth, and harmony in diversity, as shown in the mingling of ideas from Confucianism, Taoism and Buddhism and the remarkable absence of religious wars over its long history. Chinese culture is more inclusive than exclusive, which has affected all aspects of Chinese life. For instance, China's thousands of dialects have been unified under the same written language across this vast country. The people of Beijing, Shanghai and Guangzhou (Canton), the three most famous cities in China, also differ a great deal from each other in terms of lifestyle and mentality, and this difference may be even larger than between the British, the French and the German and differences among China's 56 ethnic groups are also conspicuous. But most of these differences, if not all, are made complementary to each other within the broad framework of the Confucian idea of "unity in diversity".

With the rise of China, Chinese culture is witnessing a renaissance, and the depth, width and strength of this renaissance can only be achieved in a country with such cultural richness and diversity. This renaissance is reflected in the rising "fever" for all kinds of Chinese cultural manifestations such as the ancient classics by Confucius, Mencius and Lao Tzu, Chinese paintings and calligraphy, old furniture, traditional houses, old cultural relics, Chinese medicine and Chinese traditional healthcare.

Three decades of cultural encounters with the West have not caused a loss of confidence in Chinese culture. On the contrary, these encounters have generated greater interest in China's own culture. And this is significant. Chinese culture has not been weakened by its extensive exposure to Western culture. On the contrary, it has been enriched by this exposure. The Internet is from the West, but on the Internet, there are all kinds of Chinese stories and themes ranging from *Romance of the Three Kingdoms* to *The Story of the Water Margin*, and in the age of the Internet and Twitter, China's diverse cultural heritage is the richest source of the arts and other creative activities for the Chinese.

Recent years have also witnessed the vigorous growth of China's films and TV series, and behind this growth is the wealth of stories from China's long history. Eventually, China may develop the world's largest cultural industry, as the country has a richer cultural heritage and more cultural resources than others, and has the world's largest audience and eventually the largest group of investors for the creative cultural industries.

There is perhaps no better example to illustrate this cultural richness than Chinese cuisine: there are eight main schools of cuisine and countless sub-schools, and each of the eight main schools is arguably richer than French cuisine in terms of content and variety. If French cuisine reflects the culture of France as a nation-state, then the richness of Chinese cuisine reflects the amalgamation of the cultural traditions of "hundreds of states" over China's long and continuous history. Indeed, this analogy is applicable to many other cross-cultural comparisons, and China enjoys a significantly higher degree of cultural richness and diversity than most other countries. Thanks to its continuous civilization of several millennia and its three decades of successful reform and opening up, China is now witnessing its cultural renaissance.

(5) *Unique Language*

The Chinese language is both an ancient and living language, a product of China's long history and culture. Chinese characters first evolved during the Shang Dynasty around 16 BC, when "the great city-states of classical Greece had not yet emerged, and Rome was millennia away. Yet the direct descendant of the Shang writing system is still used by well over a billion people today," as noted by Henry Kissinger.[6]

Many developing countries unfortunately lost their own languages under colonialism, and hence lost a large part of their cultural heritage and national identity. As a result, these countries often find themselves in a dilemma: on the one hand, they have lost lots of their own heritage, and on the other, their attempt to copy the Western system has failed to deliver the results they desire, and the fate of these countries seems to be forever shaped by others, and they often end up in dire poverty and prolonged chaos.

In China's state-building process, the Chinese language has kept up with the changing times. It has drawn on elements from other cultures and languages, and the language has thus undergone many "reforms": Chinese

---

[6] Henry Kissinger, *On China*, Penguin, New York, 2011, p. 6.

characters have been simplified; modern vernacular Chinese has been adopted; and the pinyin or the Latinized phonetic system has been applied. All this has facilitated the learning and use of the Chinese language. Works of human knowledge from the outside world are now all translatable, and the Chinese language is compatible with the fast progress of science and information technology. It has in fact unique advantages: unparalleled brevity, imagery and embedded cultural meanings that few other languages can match.

The Chinese language is a major source of China's vast cultural heritage, and it is used by more people than any other languages. Its influence will further grow with China's growing engagement with the outside world. The fast spread of Confucian Institutes across the world seems to show that the Chinese language is becoming a major source of China's soft power.

Many Chinese are concerned with what they perceive as the moral decay of the Chinese society due to the market-oriented economic reform, and argue that the Chinese seemingly lack some religious spirit. But religion may not be the right solution for China. Anyone with a little knowledge of world history knows that religious wars between Christians and Muslims, between various Christian denominations, have had a huge toll on human life, and religious conflicts still affect much of the world today. It is true that the Chinese society has always been more secular than religious in its long history, but it is also true that Chinese culture, influenced by Confucianism, is moralistic and humanistic, and this morality and humanism are embedded in the Chinese language. Anyone who has mastered a hundred or so Chinese idioms or proverbs learns the basic tenets of Chinese culture with all its morality and expected code of behavior, and such idioms are numerous such as *yurenweishan* (to bear kind intentions towards others), *zishiqili* (to earn one's salt), *qinjianchijia* (to be industrious and thrifty), *ziqiangbuxi* (to make unremitting efforts to improve oneself), *haoxuebujuan* (to be never tired of learning) and *tongzhougongji* (to pull together in times of trouble). Only when one travels across the world does one begin to appreciate how invaluable these tenets are. The lack of them in some cultures, to my mind, largely explains the failures of many societies and countries in the world. What one should do in China today is to revitalize the Chinese values embedded in the Chinese language through education, and in this way the Chinese society will become more harmonious and humanistic.

(6) *Unique Politics*

A civilizational state with the aforementioned "four supers" entails a unique structure and statecraft for political governance, and the governance of such a state can only be based mainly on its own methods shaped by its own traditions and culture. Henry Kissinger is right to observe that "China is singular. No other country can claim so long a continuous civilization, or such an intimate link to its ancient past and classical principles of strategy and statesmanship".[7]

In China's long history, all governments are expected to show special concern for improving people's livelihood, tackle natural and man-made disasters and cope with all the challenges posed by China's huge population and vast territory. Otherwise, it will lose the "mandate of heaven". Over the past millennia, the Chinese have shaped a political culture characterized by a longer-term vision and a more holistic way of perceiving politics. Most Chinese tend to value highly their country's overall stability and prosperity. It is unimaginable that most Chinese would ever accept the so-called multi-party democratic system with a change of central government every four years, and furthermore, all prosperous dynasties in the Chinese history were associated with a strong and enlightened state.

The Communist Party of China (CPC) is not a party as the concept "party" is understood in the West. In essence, the CPC continues the long tradition of a unified Confucian ruling entity, which represents or tries to represent the interest of the whole society, rather than a Western-style political party which openly represents group interests. The civilizational state is the product of "hundreds of states" amalgamated together over the past millennia, and if the Western political system were applied to this kind of state, its prospect could be chaos and even disintegration. The experience of China's Republican Revolution of 1911 serves to illustrate this point. The Revolution copied the Western political model and the whole country immediately fell into chaos and disintegration, with warlords, each supported by one or a few foreign powers, fighting each other for their own interests, and this is a lesson that we should always bear in mind.

---

[7] Henry Kissinger, *On China*, Penguin, New York, 2011, p. 2.

Some in the West only acknowledge the regime legitimacy bestowed by one-person-one-vote and multi-party elections, and this is shallow in the sense that if this criterion were applied, then no US government would have any claim to legitimacy prior to the mid-1960s, as most black people were not able to exercise their right to vote until the Civil Rights movement. I once encountered an American scholar questioning the legitimacy of the Chinese regime, and I suggested that he first question the legitimacy of the United States as a country: today's United States came into being following colonialism, large-scale migration from Europe and ethnic cleansing of the indigenous Indian population. From the Chinese point of view or from the view of contemporary international law, neither colonialism nor ethnic cleansing can constitute legitimacy. In the end, he agreed that all this was part of history; in other words, it is history that has shaped and determined the way legitimacy is established. This is indeed true throughout human history.

In the case of China, political ideas and practices over the past millennia are the most important source of the Chinese perception of legitimacy. The Chinese concept of legitimacy had taken shape well before modern Western states came into being. The Chinese historical discourse on regime legitimacy hinges on two key concepts. One is *minxin xiangbei* (its approximate English equivalent would be "winning or losing the hearts and minds of the people") and the other is *xuanxian renneng* (selection of talents based on meritocracy). This idea of regime legitimacy largely explains why China was a more advanced and better-governed country than the European states for the most part of the past two millennia, and why China was able to reemerge since 1978 under new circumstances. To my mind, the two concepts have embodied the collective wisdom of a civilizational state and constitute a core part of the competitiveness of the China model in its competition with the Western model.

One could well apply the Chinese concept of "selection of talents based on meritocracy" to the Western society and question the Western concept of legitimacy. Without this legitimacy based on meritocracy, how could a regime be qualified to govern? How could such a regime be accountable to its people and to the world? This is illustrated by the example of the presidency of George W. Bush, and his eight years of incompetence caused huge damage to the interests of the American and other peoples as shown in the financial crisis and the Iraq War.

China's political, economic and social systems are also more inclusive. Over China's long history, multiple political, economic and social systems overlapped each other and co-existed, and such systems ranged from the "county and prefecture system" to the "tributary system" to the "suzerain-vassal system" to the "system of autonomous entities", and this variety and inclusiveness are rare for Western-style nation-states. In today's China, there are the "one-country-two-systems" models of Hong Kong and Macau, autonomous regions for ethnic minorities, and special economic institutional arrangements with Hong Kong, Macau and Taiwan under various names. Since three decades ago, China has encouraged some regions to become prosperous first, to be followed by other regions, and this strategy is difficult to conceive in other countries with different political cultural traditions. But in China, thanks to its unique political traditions, this initiative has produced the remarkable $1 + 1 > 2$ effect.

Other Chinese political concepts, such as "when one region is in trouble, all other regions will come to help" (*yifangyounan bafangzhiyuan*) and "the whole country is treated as a single chessboard" (*quanguo yipanqi*), which means the coordination of all the major initiatives of the nation like moves on a single chessboard, are indeed rare in most other countries with different political cultures or systems. I once discussed the China model with some Indian scholars, who observed that on the surface, the Chinese political system represents a lot of concentration of power, but in reality, all reforms in China have their strong local flavors and different regions in China both compete and cooperate with each other, and that the Chinese system is much more dynamic and flexible than the Indian one. Indeed, if one takes the three regions of the Yangtze River Delta as an example, one finds that the functions of the state, market and society differ from each other in the economies of Shanghai, Jiangsu and Zhejiang. And this diversity mirrors in fact that of the whole country where intra-regional competition and cooperation thrive, and China's rapid reemergence to a great extent can be attributed to this combination of competition and cooperation at local levels.

In short, China has learnt a lot from the West in order to create a powerful modern state. At the same time, China retains, intentionally or unintentionally, many of its political cultural traditions. This has allowed China today to be in a seemingly better position to overcome many challenges that the Western model is experiencing, such as simple-minded populism, short-termism and excessive legalism. With the passage of time, the Chinese political wisdom is likely to generate an ever greater impact on the rest of the world.

(7) *Unique Society*

The traditional society of China was based on family and kinships, and the Chinese ancestors were mainly settled "farmers" engaged in agricultural activities, in which family and kinships played a uniquely important role. In contrast, the Western society is more individual-oriented as it started, in most cases, from a nomadic existence in which blood relationship was less emphasized. In this sense, the Chinese and the Western societies constitute two different types of societies. In contrast to the individual-based Western society, the Chinese one is far more family-based and group-oriented, and this structure is further extended into a whole set of social norms and relationships and reflected in the Chinese way of life.

Over the past millennia, there also emerged such prevalent Chinese ideas as *sheji weijia* (sacrificing oneself for one's family) and *baojia weiguo* (defending one's family and safeguarding one's nation), which have shaped what is called *jiaguo tonggou* or "family and nation in one", as implied by the Chinese characters for the word "nation" which is composed of the two characters "state" (国) and "family" (家). This linkage of an individual's pursuit with a broader and higher social commitment is a core idea of Confucianism, and Confucius famously wrote, "cultivating one's moral character, putting one's house in order, running the country well and letting peace prevail under the heaven". In the process of building a modern state, this old Confucian value has gradually evolved into people's strong sense of identity with the Chinese nation and with its overall cohesiveness.

With the rapid pace of modernization, China's social structure has undergone a fast transformation. The old subsistence economy and low-mobility society have been replaced by a fast-changing and most mobile society connected with the outside world. People's lifestyles have undergone rapid changes accordingly. In the process, it seems that every individual or every cell of the society has been mobilized for self-fulfillment, for making money, for greater achievement, and the Chinese society is thus extremely dynamic and full of competition and opportunities. Yet, with such a fast-changing society, tensions of all sorts have also surfaced, a situation similar to that of an adolescent with all the hopes and risks that his or her age entails. But from a broader historical perspective, this stage of development may be inevitable as a society moves towards modernization.

With the quickened pace of modernization, it is widely thought that individual-based and self-centered Western values may replace China's family-based values. Yet the reality is different. While many traditional Chinese values have indeed been eroded with China's rapid pace of modernization, the process has also witnessed a growing and ever stronger desire to return to Chinese roots and to embrace some core Chinese values, and this is happening in today's entirely new environment, as China is now widely open to the outside world. There is no better example to illustrate this trend than the Chinese pop song "Coming Home More Often" (*Chang huijia kankan*) which became a national hit overnight a few years back. It apparently struck a chord with most Chinese people: whatever social and economic changes in China, family remains the core of emotional attachment for most Chinese, and filial piety, however diluted when judged by the traditional Chinese standards, remains crucial for the Chinese. In today's China, individual freedoms have been expanded a great many times, yet most people are still ready to make sacrifices for their families to a degree that individual-based Westerners will find it difficult to comprehend. This is also the main reason why Chinese society tends to be more cohesive than most Western societies. In today's China, the culture of filial piety seems to go along exceedingly well with the expansion of individual rights and freedoms.

In the political domain, some in the West take it for granted that with the rise of China's middle class, the Chinese society will also follow the Western model and end in conflicts between society and state. But they seem to have discovered that in China today the middle class, more than any other class, is a staunch force for China's political stability. China's middle class is made up largely of well-educated people who tend to appreciate China's stability, and they are more aware of the fact that China has experienced too much *luan* or chaos in its history and Western-style democratization has brought about too much *luan* in other parts of the world and that their hard-won wealth is inseparable from China's continuous stability over the past three decades. Looking into the future, China's overall social trends are more likely to follow a model of mutually complementary interactions between society and state, rather than the Western model of confrontation between society and state.

(8) *Unique Economy*

In China's long history, economics was, strictly speaking, not market economics, but humanistic economics. In other words, it was always more political economics than pure economics. Chinese traditional economics tended to link economic development with political governance and link the improvement of people's living standards with the country's overall stability, rather than profit maximization. Influenced by this tradition, the guidelines for China's development today are "human-centered development" and "satisfying people's demands". In Chinese history, if the state failed to develop the economy and improve people's living standards or cope with major natural calamities, it would lose the hearts and minds of the people and hence lose the "mandate of heaven".

From my point of view, the Chinese concept of the "socialist market economy" today is in essence a mix of Western market economics and China's traditional humanistic economics. Neither market economics nor humanistic economics on its own can work well in China, as the former alone can hardly meet the demands of the general population whose expectation of the state is always high, while the latter alone does not allow China to compete on the world stage. To my mind, the China model today has combined both the strengths of market economics and humanistic economics, and this combination has produced the competitiveness of the Chinese economy.

In the Chinese tradition of economic development over the past millennia, the visible hand of state intervention was always present, as seen in the debate over the government monopoly of salt and iron in the Western Han Dynasty (202 BC to AD 9) or the Self-Strengthening Movement in the second half of the 19th century. Judging from the experience of reform and opening up over the past three decades, it is fair to argue that if one had only relied on the spontaneous market signals without a strong state to promote and organize various market-oriented reform initiatives, it would have taken a much longer time to establish a market economy with a sound foundation and regulation in China.

Thanks to three decades of unremitting efforts, China's socialist market economy has largely taken shape, which combines what the Chinese American historian Ray Huang called "numerical management" (or micro management) with what can be called "macro regulation", and created a highly competitive economy in the world. "Numerical management" is the strength of the West, and China has learnt to master it to a great extent, but "macro regulation" is rooted in Chinese culture and it is the strength of China, and the West has not yet realized that it would serve its own interest to learn something from China in this regard. It is also true that given the individual-oriented culture and traditions, it may not be all that easy for the West to do so. To my mind, with intensified globalization and international competition, an economy with only the competence of "numerical management", not "macro regulation", may not be as competitive as those with both competences. I will elaborate on this in the next chapter on China's development model.

In summary, China itself is a splendid universe. As mentioned earlier, if the ancient Egyptian, Mesopotamian, Indus Valley and Greek civilizations had continued to this day and undergone a process of modern state transformation, then they could also be civilizational states; if the ancient Roman empire had not disintegrated and been able to accomplish the transformation into a modern state, then today's Europe could also be a medium-sized civilizational state; if the Islamic world today made up of dozens of countries could become unified under one modern governing regime, it could also be a civilizational state with more than a billion people, but the chance for all these scenarios has long gone, and in the world today, China is the sole country where the world's longest continuous civilization and a modern state are merged into one.

Frankly speaking, the world's longest continuous civilization itself is precious and invaluable, with all its tangible and intangible legacies of mankind and their implications for the future, and one should treat this civilization with due respect. The Chinese civilization today is both old and young and full of dynamism. Its manifestations cannot and should not be assessed by over-simplistic dichotomies of "modern" or "backward", "democratic" or "autocratic", "high human rights standards" or "low human rights standards", as contended by some Chinese and Western scholars. The contents of the Chinese civilization are 100 of times more complicated and sophisticated than what these shallow concepts are able to capture. Indeed, a civilization that has been sustained for more than 5,000 years must contain some unique wisdom, and we should treat it the same way as we treat other tangible and intangible cultural legacies of mankind, some of which have already become the spiritual and intellectual sources powering China's decisive move beyond the Western model.

The civilizational state is both one state and "hundreds of states in one". As one state, it is characterized by an unparalleled cohesive strength and competence for macro governance, and as "hundreds of states in one", it is marked by the greatest internal diversity, yet as a part of China's continuous civilization for millennia, this diversity works well under the Confucian idea of "unity in diversity".

3.3 A New Perspective

Under the China model, the four features of the civilizational state (population, territory, tradition and culture) all constitute China's greatest strengths. China has the richest human resources and potentially the largest consumer market; China has an unparalleled geopolitical and geoeconomic status; China has its own tradition of independent thinking, and has the richest cultural resources in the world. However, if China abandons its own model and adopts the Western model, then the greatest strengths of China as a civilizational state may turn out to be its greatest weaknesses. "Hundreds of states in one" may become "hundreds of states in conflict"; its emphasis on harmonious politics may become adversarial politics; its huge population a rich source of contentions; its unified vast territory split and disintegrate; and its diverse traditions the pretext for endless disputes and its cultural richness the source of cultural clashes. And the dream of the Chinese nation's renaissance may well perish.

Due to the nature of the civilizational state, China cannot and should not copy the Western model, and China should be selective in its learning from the outside world, as has been the case over the past three decades. Under no circumstances should China lose its own identity and inherent strengths. For instance, the mainstream view in the West argues that the market economy should be based on private ownership of land, yet China is a large and populous country with limited arable land, and mishandling of land always led to economic and social crises in China's long history. China's land system today has combined the public ownership of land with the individual right to use the land, and this innovative approach has proven to be a core part of China's overall competitiveness. Without this kind of innovative system, how could China, within so short a period of time, build up a first-rate infrastructure, carry out a large-scale urban facelift across the country, and allow the Chinese home ownership to become one of the highest in the world? Naturally, the Chinese land system has its share of problems which should be addressed step by step, but its future remains bright, and abandoning it would be foolish.

In a broad sense, China and the West can exchange ideas and practices for each other's benefit, and China has been doing so over the past three decades, but at a deeper level there are things that should not and cannot be changed, as they constitute the essence of a nation, distinguishing it from other nations, and efforts to change the essence of China is likely to end up in complete failure.

The political tradition of a nation has its own internal logic and a nation should evolve along its own internal logic, rather than pursuing political romanticism which could be extremely costly for a super-large country like China. In fact, even a country like Britain, which has a much shorter history than China, has all along adhered to its own political traditions and never accepted the French type of democracy then prevalent in much of Europe. I even wonder if the European Union, with only one third of China's population, could function if it were to be governed under today's prevailing system in the West, i.e. popular election and a multi-party system. If the European Union adopted this model, it would either degenerate into a symbolic white elephant without the ability to promote Europe's collective interests or fall into disarray and end up in disintegration.

The greatest wisdom of a civilizational state is perhaps its long tradition of "seeking common ground while reserving differences", and this wisdom is first of all reflected in the Chinese language. Chinese characters are commonly made up of various components, and the components often give a hint of the pronunciation and the meaning of the word, and they are structured in such a way that they often follow the principle of "seeking common ground while reserving differences". For instance, virtually all words relating to water contain a component indicating water, as shown in the Chinese characters for river (江), lake (湖), sea (海) and ocean (洋), and virtually all words relating to metal contain a component indicating metal, as shown in silver (银), copper (铜), iron (铁) and tin (锡). German philosopher Martin Heidegger famously said that it is not that "we speak the language, but the language speaks us", i.e. the language we use actually reflects our way of thinking and behaving. The Chinese language seems to underline the fact that seeking commonality from diversity is a trait of Chinese culture. Hence, the core vocabulary of the Chinese language is much smaller than any European languages. Reading Chinese newspapers requires mastering about 3,000 characters, which then take all kinds of combinations to express countless meanings. In contrast, Western languages tend to focus on seeking differences, and hence have a much larger core vocabulary.

To my mind, the governance of a civilizational state follows the same logic, and if one can focus on seeking the commonalities of different interest groups, one stands a better chance of solving the tensions among them, whether it is the tension between regions, between enterprises, between social groups or between rich and poor. If one shifts away from the China model of seeking commonalities to the Western model of stressing differences, it is more likely to lead to social instability and conflicts.

The concept of a civilizational state can prompt us to rethink many preconceived concepts, for instance per capita GDP as a measurement of the level of development for cross-country comparisons. In fact, such comparisons could be misleading with regard to countries of different sizes and natures. A symphony orchestra made up of several hundreds of players can hardly be compared with a single violinist, pianist or a chamber music group. Norway's per capita GDP is much higher than China's, but China has thousands of industries that Norway does not have. If comparison has to be made, it is perhaps more pertinent to compare two violinists, say, Norway, with a population of 5 million, and Suzhou, a city near Shanghai with a population of 8 million. This kind of comparison may be more relevant and immediately comprehensible for people directly concerned. After all, a heavyweight boxer and a lightweight boxer are hardly comparable and they can not be equalized by the average method, as they belong to different categories of sportsmen. And if boxers cannot be compared by the average method, how can cross-country comparisons be made and become genuinely relevant when intra-country differences are 1,000 times more complicated than boxing?

China is indeed too big, and its geographical, economic, social, political and cultural spaces are simply too huge to be compared with most other states. China's population is four times that of the US, and it is not far-fetched to say, at least in theory, that it is only normal that there are four times more problems in China than in the US, although in fact, problems are perhaps fewer in China than in the US, as shown by the fact that the US's prison population is larger than China's.

Another example is the measurement of the number of outbound tourists as an indication of change in living standards. China is a super-large civilizational state, and it is "hundreds of states in one". When one travels from Austria via Slovakia to Hungary and the Czech Republic, it is almost like traveling from Shanghai to Nanjing with short stopovers in Suzhou and Wuxi. If we have to apply the measurement of outbound tourists for international comparisons, it is perhaps more accurate to consider all those Chinese who take planes or high-speed trains within this huge country. There were 30 million outbound trips from South Korea in 2009 and 60 million from China in the same year. But South Korea is a small country, and once you embark on a plane, you may go abroad. On the surface, China's outbound tourists only double South Korea's, but in reality the number of Chinese with such means to travel abroad are at least five to ten times higher.

Likewise, when one treats the Western countries not as single countries but as part of the Western civilization, one acquires a sharper perspective of history, culture and reality, and it becomes easier for us to discover the innate strengths as well as weaknesses of a civilization, and to know how to better understand and deal with the West and to increase one's self-confidence. If one compares the evolutions of the Chinese and Western civilizations, one will find that the rise of the West is not simply a process of industrialization, urbanization, globalization and democratization, but also a process of slavery, colonialism, fascism, ethnic cleansing, the outbreak of world wars, and bullying and exploiting many other nations. Among the Western countries, there are less corrupt ones like the Nordic countries, but there are also corrupt ones like Greece and Italy. One will also discover the long-term historical trends of China and the West: China led the world for most of the time in the past 2,000 years, started lagging behind the West from the 18th century, and then began to catch up with the West three decades ago.

The Chinese civilization is the world's longest continuous civilization and it seems capable of drawing on positive elements from other civilizations while retaining its own identity, just like Indian Buddhism being Sinicized, and Marxism too. Now, 400 million Chinese are learning English, 20% of Chinese publications every year are translated books, and China's newspaper with the largest circulation is *Reference News*, a daily translation of foreign press news and comments. McDonald's meets resistance in many countries, but not in China. The objective of the Chinese seems clear: they want to learn from others and eventually do better, and though such efforts may not always succeed, they never cease.

In certain ways, one may argue that the three decades of reform constitute an effort to let the Chinese civilization face global competition to see if it can withstand such competition. It seems that it has withstood the test of international competition, and its core contents have been revitalized and China has thus become one of the most dynamic countries in the world, and this unique civilizational state is bound to generate its impact on the future evolution of the world economic and political order.

3.4 Looking at China Afresh

On January 18, 2009, former Finnish president and Nobel laureate Martti Ahtisaari chaired a seminar in Brussels on crisis management in Africa and I was invited to speak on the China model. In the evening, the Finnish ambassador to the European Union held a dinner for the participants of the seminar. When Ahtisaari stood up to speak, he said that many issues in Africa today call for new ideas and solutions, and he reflected a bit on my presentation on the China model and came to the conclusion that the Political Bureau of the Communist Party of China was like the board of directors of a corporation, the general secretary of the Party was like the chairman of the board, the premier was like the CEO of the corporation and the governance of China was more or less like managing a company. He asked me to give a response. I said, "Indeed, we have reflected on this question. Why do no companies in the world elect its CEO through one-person-one-vote? If it is done this way, the company may risk bankruptcy. Likewise, in terms of political system, we should consider how a country can be best governed. To my mind, the essence of democracy is the will of the people and good governance of a country, rather than democracy for the sake of democracy, or election for the sake of election."

Sitting next to me was European strategist Robert G. Cooper. He was not entirely satisfied with my reply and asked, "Do you mean that China does not accept Lincoln's idea of 'government of the people, by the people, for the people?'" I replied, "We do value these principles, but we also have our own political traditions, the essence of which is two concepts: one is to 'win the hearts and minds of the people' and the other is meritocracy. In other words, a country, in our political traditions, must be governed by talents with expertise in running state affairs selected on the basis of meritocracy." President Ahtisaari observed, "I visited China many times and often told my friends that China is different from the Soviet Union and it is an ancient civilization and it has its own approaches to many issues, and one should be able to draw on Chinese wisdom."

A scholar from Central Africa present concurred with my view and quipped, "I agree that the key to success of a country is the quality of its leaders, and a joke in my country goes like this: The rich endowments of Central Africa aroused envy in all its neighbors, who then went to God and asked Him why He had given all the valuable resources to Central Africa, not them. God's reply was simple and straightforward: 'Don't worry, I've given everything to Central Africa, except good leaders.'" Everyone laughed and the dinner turned out to be an occasion to discuss how to better understand China and Africa.

With the rise of China, how to really understand this country has drawn international attention. For instance, *Time Magazine* published an interesting article titled "Five Things the US Can Learn from China", authored by Bill Powell, in November 2009. The article notes that President

Obama's visit to China "comes at an awkward moment for the US" and China,

> despite its 5,000-year burden of history, has emerged as a dynamo of optimism, experimentation and growth. It has defied the global economic slump, and the sense that it's the world's ascendant power has never been stronger. The US, by contrast, seems suddenly older and frailer. America's national mood is still in a funk, its economy foundering, its red-vs.-blue politics as rancorous as ever. The US may be one of the world's oldest capitalist countries and China one of the youngest, but you couldn't blame Obama if he leaned over to Hu at some point and asked, "What are you guys doing right?"

Powell lists the following five things that the US can learn from China:

(1) *Be Ambitious*

Powell writes that the United States is

> close to tapped out financially, with budget deficits this year and next exceeding $1 trillion and forecast to remain above $500 billion through 2019. But sometimes the country seems tapped out in terms of vision and investment for the future. What's palpable in China is the sense of forward motion, of energy. There's no direct translation into Chinese of the phrase can-do spirit. But *yong wang zhi qian* probably suffices. Literally, it means "march forward courageously." China has — and has had for years now — a can-do spirit that's unmistakable.

He quotes the words of James McGregor, former chairman of the American Chamber of Commerce in China:

> "One key thing we can learn from China is setting goals, making plans and focusing on moving the country ahead as a nation," he says. "These guys have taken the old five-year plans and stood them on their head. Instead of deciding which factory gets which raw materials, which prod-

ucts are made, how they are priced and where they are sold, their
planning now consists of 'How do we build a world-class silicon-chip
industry in five years? How do we become a global player in car-
manufacturing?'"

(2) *Education Matters*

Although China "doesn't produce many Nobel Prize winners", as Powell
claims, China invests heavily in the basic education of the workforce:

> After decades of investment in an educational system that reaches the
> remotest peasant villages, the literacy rate in China is now over 90%.
> (The U.S.'s is 86%.) And in urban China, in particular, students don't just
> learn to read. They learn math. They learn science.

The article claims that

> fundamentally, they are getting the basics right, particularly in math
> and science. We need to do the same. Their kids are often ahead of
> ours.

And

> it all starts with the emphasis families put on the importance of edu-
> cation. That puts pressure on the government to deliver a decent
> system.

(3) *Look After the Elderly*

The author notes the huge difference between the two societies with regard
to dealing with their elderly:

> And I can vouch for that firsthand. My wife Junling is a Shanghai
> native, and last month for the first time we visited my father at a nurs-
> ing home in the US. She was shaken by the experience and later told
> me, "You know, in China, it's a great shame to put a parent into a nurs-
> ing home." In China the social contract has been straightforward for
> centuries: parents raise children; then the children care for the parents

as they reach their old age. When, for example, real estate developer Jiang Xiao Li and his wife recently bought a new, larger apartment in Shanghai, they did so in part because they know that in a few years, his parents will move in with them. Jiang's parents will help take care of Jiang's daughter, and as they age, Jiang and his wife will help take care of them. As China slowly develops a better-funded and more reliable social-security system for retirees — which it has begun — the economic necessity of generations living together will diminish a bit. But no one believes that as China gets richer, the cultural norm will shift too significantly.

The author notes,

> grandparents tutor young children while Mom and Dad work; they acculturate the youngest generation to the values of family and nation; they provide a sense of cultural continuity that helps bind a society. China needs to make obvious changes to its elder-care system as it becomes a wealthier society, but as millions of US families make the brutal decision about whether to send aging parents into nursing homes, a bigger dose of the Chinese ethos may well be returning to America.

(4) *Save More*

Powell also highlights the high savings rate in China and its many benefits for the country:

> China, like many other East Asian countries, is a society that has esteemed personal financial prudence for centuries. There is no chance that will change anytime soon, even if the government creates a better social safety net and successfully encourages greater consumer spending. Why does the US need to learn a little frugality? Because healthy savings rates, including government and business savings, are one of the surest indicators of a country's long-term financial health. High savings lead, over time, to increased investment, which in turn generates productivity gains, innovation and job growth. In short, savings are the seed corn of a good economic harvest.

(5) *Look over the Horizon*

The author writes with appreciation that so many Chinese have changed their fate through their own efforts in "a forward looking country" and he quotes

> a smart American who lived in China for years and who wants to avoid being identified publicly (perhaps because he'd be labeled a "panda hugger," the timeworn epithet tossed at anyone who has anything good to say about China) puts it this way: "China is striving to become what it has not yet become. It is upwardly mobile, consciously, avowedly and — as its track record continues to strengthen — proudly so."

And

> if that sounds familiar to Americans — marooned, for the moment, in the deepest recession in 26 years — it should.[8]

The five things listed by Powell are all manifestations of China as a civilizational state: being ambitious to plan and carry out big projects reflects the nature of China's strong and pro-modernization state; China's emphasis on education reveals the Confucian tradition of valuing the importance of learning; looking after the elderly is a continuation of Chinese family values with an emphasis on filial piety; the high savings rate shows the Chinese tradition of appreciating industriousness and thrift; and looking over the horizon recalls the famous lines contained in the *I Ching* written over 2,000 years ago: "As Heaven's movement is ever vigorous, so must a gentleman ceaselessly strive along." And it also attests to the Confucian tradition of "selecting talents irrespective of their family background".

New York Times columnist Roger Cohen also published an op-ed piece in January 2011 titled "Single-Party Democracy", which deserves to be quoted at length here:

> I'm bullish on China after a couple of weeks here and perhaps that sentiment begins with the little emperors and empresses. In upscale

---

[8] Bill Powell, "Five Things the US Can Learn from China", *Time Magazine*, November 13, 2009.

city parks and rundown urban sprawls, I've seen China's children pampered by grandparents, coddled by fathers, cared for by extended families.

Scarcity may explain the doting: China's one-child policy makes children special. But there are deeper forces at work. The race for modernity has not blown apart the family unit, whatever the strains. After witnessing the atomization of American society, where the old are often left to fend for themselves, China feels cohesive.

It's seeing that most natural of conspiracies — between grandparents and children — flourishing. It's listening to young women in coastal factories talking about sending half their salaries home to some village in Guangxi where perhaps it goes to build a second floor on a parental house. It's hearing young couples agonize over whether they can afford a child because "affording" means school, possible graduate education abroad, and a deposit on the first apartment.

The family is at once emotional bedrock and social insurance. "My" money equals my family's money. All the parental investment reaps a return in the form of care later in life. "Children are a retirement fund," a Chinese-American friend living here told me. "If you don't have children, what do you do in old age?"

The Chinese, in other words, might be lining up to play karaoke after long factory shifts, but they're not bowling alone American-style. They're not stressing because they're all alone. That's critical. There so much heaving change here — China's planning to open 97 new airports and 83 subway systems in the next five years — the family strikes me as the great stabilizer (even more than the regime's iron fist).

As Arthur Kroeber, an economist, said, "High-growth stories are not pretty. If you're growing at 10 percent a year, a lot of stuff gets knocked down." It sure does: China looms through the dust. But the family has proved resilient, cushioning life for the have-nots, offering a moral compass for the haves (rampant corruption notwithstanding).

After the emperors and empresses, in my bullish assessment, comes the undistracted forward focus. After a while in Asia, you notice the absence of a certain background noise. It's as if you've removed a negative drone from your life, like the slightly startled relief you feel when the hum of an air conditioner ceases.

What's in that American drone? Oh, the wars of course, the cost of them, and debate around them, and the chatter surrounding terror and fear. There's also the resentment-infused aftermath of the great financial meltdown, navigated by China with an adroitness that helped salvage the world economy from oblivion. In the place of all that Western angst, there's growth, growth, growth, which tends (through whatever ambivalence) to inspire awe rather than dread. The world's center of gravity is shifting with a seismic inevitability.

I know, China has kept its foot on the gas of its stimulus package too long and there are bubble signs in housing and labor is no longer limitless, with resultant inflationary pressure. I also know there are tensions between state economic direction and market forces, with resultant waste. But my third bullish element is nonetheless an economy entering a 15-year sweet spot where rising disposable income will drive the domestic market.

Think of what Japan, Taiwan and South Korea went through decades ago, but with a population of 1.3 billion. Think of the 10 to 15 million new urban residents a year and the homes and infrastructure they will need. Think of all the stuff the world demands and can't get elsewhere with the same quality, quantity and price. Think underlying drivers. They remain powerful.

Of course, political upheaval could unhinge all the above. Given that China's open-closed experiment is unique in history, nobody can say how this society will be governed in 2050. Immense tensions, not least between the rage that corruption inspires and the difficulty of tackling it without a free press, exist. Still, my fourth reason for running with the Chinese bulls is perhaps the most surprising: single-party democracy.

It doesn't exist. It's an oxymoron (although a US primary is a vote within one party). It can easily be the semantic disguise for outrage and oppression. But it just may be the most important political idea of the 21st century. Rightful resistance is growing in China. Citizens are asserting their rights, not in organizing against the state (dangerous) but in using laws to have a say. Nongovernmental organizations are multiplying to advance agendas from the environment to labor rights. This is happening with the acquiescence of smart rulers.

"They know they cannot manage in the old way," Ma Jun, a leading environmentalist, told me. "They cannot dam the water, but they can go with the flow and divert it to the places they want." Whether that place will ever resemble one-party democracy, I don't know. But I no longer laugh at the idea. Harmonious discord is an old Chinese idea. The extended Chinese family is a daily exercise in just that.[9]

Another thought-provoking op-ed article was written by Robert J. Herbold, a retired chief operating officer of Microsoft Corporation, titled "China vs. America: Which Is the Developing Country?", carried in *The Wall Street Journal* on July 9, 2011. The author compared the two countries in the following way:

Infrastructure: Let's face it, Los Angeles is decaying. Its airport is cramped and dirty, too small for the volume it tries to handle and in a state of disrepair. In contrast, the airports in Beijing and Shanghai are brand new, clean and incredibly spacious, with friendly, courteous staff galore. They are extremely well-designed to handle the large volume of air traffic needed to carry out global business these days.

In traveling the highways around Los Angeles to get to the airport, you are struck by the state of disrepair there, too. Of course, everyone knows California is bankrupt and that is probably the reason why. In contrast, the infrastructure in the major Chinese cities such as Shanghai and Beijing is absolute state-of-the-art and relatively new.

The congestion in the two cities is similar. In China, consumers are buying 18 million cars per year compared to 11 million in the US. China is working hard building roads to keep up with the gigantic demand for the automobile.

The just-completed Beijing to Shanghai high-speed rail link, which takes less than five hours for the 800-mile trip, is the crown jewel of

---

[9] Roger Cohen, "Single-Party Democracy", *The New York Times*, January 21, 2011.

China's current 5,000 miles of rail, set to grow to 10,000 miles in 2020. Compare that to decaying Amtrak.

Government Leadership: Here the differences are staggering. In every meeting we attended, with four different customers of our company as well as representatives from four different arms of the Chinese government, our hosts began their presentation with a brief discussion of China's new five-year-plan. This is the 12th five-year plan and it was announced in March 2011. Each of these groups reminded us that the new five-year plan is primarily focused on three things: (1) improving innovation in the country; (2) making significant improvements in the environmental footprint of China; and (3) continuing to create jobs to employ large numbers of people moving from rural to urban areas. Can you imagine the US Congress and president emerging with a unified five-year plan that they actually achieve (like China typically does)?

The specificity of China's goals in each element of the five-year plan is impressive. For example, China plans to cut carbon emissions by 17% by 2016. In the same time frame, China's high-tech industries are to grow to 15% of the economy from 3% today.

Government Finances: This topic is, frankly, embarrassing. China manages its economy with incredible care and is sitting on trillions of dollars of reserves. In contrast, the US government has managed its financials very poorly over the years and is flirting with a Greece-like catastrophe.

[…]

Technology and Innovation: To give you a feel for China's determination to become globally competitive in technology innovation, let me cite some statistics from two facilities we visited. Over the last 10 years, the Institute of Biophysics, an arm of the Chinese Academy of Science, has received very significant investment by the Chinese government. Today it consists of more than 3,000 talented scientists focused on doing world-class research in areas such as protein science, and brain and cognitive sciences.

We also visited the new Shanghai Advanced Research Institute, another arm of the Chinese Academy of Science. This gigantic science and technology park is under construction and today consists of four buildings, but it will grow to over 60 buildings on a large piece of land equivalent to about a third of a square mile. It is being staffed by Ph.D.-caliber researchers. Their goal statement is fairly straightforward: "To be a pioneer in the development of new technologies relevant to business."

All of the various institutes being run by the Chinese Academy of Science are going to be significantly increased in size, and staffing will be aided by a new recruiting program called "Ten Thousand Talents." This is an effort by the Chinese government to reach out to Chinese individuals who have been trained, and currently reside, outside China. They are focusing on those who are world-class in their technical abilities, primarily at the Ph.D. level, at work in various universities and science institutes abroad. In each year of this new five-year plan, the goal is to recruit 2,000 of these individuals to return to China.

Reasons and Cure: Given all of the above, I think you can see why I pose the fundamental question: Which is the developing country and which is the developed country? The next questions are: Why is this occurring and what should the US do? [...] What is the cure? Washington politicians and American voters need to snap to and realize they are getting beaten — and make big changes that put the US back on track: Fix the budget and the burden of entitlements; implement an aggressive five-year debt-reduction plan, and start approving some winning plans. Wake up, America![10]

Yet, to this author, it is not only "Wake up, America!" but also "Wake up, China!", as many Chinese at home are still unable to understand or appreciate the significance of the rise of their own country.

---

[10] Robert J. Herbold, "China vs. America: Which Is the Developing Country?", *The Wall Street Journal*, July 9, 2011.

CHAPTER 4

THE RISE OF A DEVELOPMENT MODEL

4.1 Reflections after the Crises

Most East Asian countries were all once under the influence of the Chinese civilization, especially its Confucian traditions and practices, and much of this region is often called the "Confucian cultural sphere" or "chopsticks cultural sphere". The Chinese model of development is naturally inseparable from the so-called East Asian model, and perhaps it is reasonable to perceive the China model as a unique extension of the East Asian model. The East Asian model mainly refers to the state-guided modernization process as shown in the case of the four Little Dragons (Singapore, Hong Kong, South Korea and Taiwan) which all share similar cultural backgrounds. Whatever problems they are still faced with, these Little Dragons have effectively modernized their economies through the East Asian model.

Similar to the Little Dragons, China has successfully pursued its modernization program while simultaneously transforming its planned economy into a socialist market economy. The rise of a super-large nation with 1.3 billion people also means that its model of development produces a scale effect unmatchable by the Little Dragons, and the China model is therefore more likely to generate a greater and more lasting impact on the world.

The East Asian model was, however, controversial during the 1997 financial crisis, and its critics also targeted criticism at the China model.

Thailand, South Korea, Indonesia and Malaysia all suffered heavy losses during the 1997 crisis. Many analysts then blamed the crisis on "crony capitalism", i.e. excessive government intervention in the economy led to the collusion of special interest groups and corrupt politicians, resulting in credit inflation, power-for-money deals and the bubble economy.

Yet it is perhaps necessary to make a distinction here: with the exception of South Korea, the aforementioned countries do not exactly fit into the East Asian model. These countries modeled themselves after the East Asian model but failed to achieve a substantive leap. Compared to the Little Dragons, their government intervention was weaker in terms of foresight, continuity and level of realism. Their American-style financial liberalization, together with the problem of crony capitalism, ultimately crashed their economies.

However, even during the debate on the cause of the crisis, many East Asian scholars highlighted "casino capitalism" instead of "crony capitalism" as the primary cause of the Asian financial crisis, during which the American and Western speculators wreaked havoc through the unsupervised financial market. In retrospect, if the US financial regulatory institutions had heeded the advice of these scholars, the current financial crisis could have been avoided.

Of the four Little Dragons, South Korea was the worst hit by the 1997 financial crisis. Its model of state-guided development can be traced back to the 1960s when the South Korean financial institutions, shadows of the government economic policy, provided loans to major corporations with close ties to the government. But from my observation, the loose control over loans was proportional to the process of democratization since 1987. Along with the South Korean democratization was a swift expansion of economic nationalism. The South Korean government rushed to invest in domestic enterprises and liberalized the capital market in the early 1990s and South Korean elite were so preoccupied with elections that the supervision of the economy was somehow neglected, and South Korea thus became the worst-hit Little Dragon during the crisis.

Nevertheless, thanks to the East Asian model, South Korea had already made a substantial economic leap prior to the 1997 crisis. A comparison between South Korea and Tanzania serves to illustrate this point. Fifty years ago, Tanzania's per capita income was slightly higher than that of

South Korea. Now, the difference between the two countries could not be bigger: South Korea is more or less a medium developed country while Tanzania is still a typical developing country. In other words, the East Asian model might have its weakness and faces many challenges, but its overall efficacy in raising people's living standards and achieving social and economic modernization is not yet matched by any other development models. This suffices to establish the historic standing of the East Asian model.

Some mainstream scholars in the West attempted to negate the East Asian model and the China model in the aftermath of the 1997 crisis, and they prescribed two solutions to the affected Asian countries at that time. First, promotion of full marketization and rejection of government intervention in the economy (though the US is doing exactly the opposite now). Second, promotion of full democratization to solve the problems of "crony capitalism". Nobel laureate in economics Amartya Sen even went as far as to say that the crisis was a penalty for countries that did not implement democracy.[1] The irony is that the current financial crisis, which is much worse than the 1997 crisis, started in the United States, a model state of democracy. Its "superior" democratic system had no inkling of the coming crisis, and its crisis management is far below the expected standards. One has to wonder how Sen would explain all this now.

I tend to believe that the overwhelming power of capital in the American political system is a major cause of the current crisis. I can further submit that, to paraphrase Sen's words, the current crisis is a penalty for those who believe in market fundamentalism and democratic fundamentalism. In fact, both the market and democracy are products of human civilizations and can be adapted by all countries according to their respective local conditions. But once a certain type of democratic model or market institution is promoted as the one and only, it is no different from religious fundamentalism, where the believers tend to lose their capacity for reason and rational thinking. The result can only be dreadful. This is the underlying cause of many issues in the world today, from the

---

[1] Amartya Sen, "Democracy as a Universal Value", *Journal of Democracy*, 10 (1999), pp. 3–17.

current financial crash to the failure of Bush's Greater Middle East Initiative.

Interestingly, South Korea and Taiwan switched to the American democratic model after achieving economic take-off with the East Asian model, but with a result far from satisfactory. The Political and Economic Risk Consultancy's (PERC) report for 2009 revealed that the level of corruption in Taiwan was higher than in the Chinese mainland. Despite the denial from some Taiwanese, it is simply true that gangs and money have engulfed Taiwanese politics, and its democratic system has been swiftly marketized after Taiwan's democratization. Ma Ying-jeou now seeks economic cooperation with Beijing in order to save Taiwan's declining economy. This is a wise option, as indeed, the Taiwanese economy has few other options. South Korea encountered a similar problem to Taiwan's after its democratization, and the country was unfortunately hit hard in both the 1997 and 2008 crises. South Korea's current recovery has been led by its close engagement with the Chinese economy which is still expanding at a rather high speed.

The issue of "crony capitalism" requires serious attention and should be resolved through institutional reforms. However, the current financial crisis has also revealed what can be called American-style financial corruption and its disastrous impact on the US itself and the world at large. American-style financial corruption may be described as "second-generation corruption". First-generation corruption is such "uncivilized" acts as hidden commissions, smuggling and briberies of the primitive type, while second-generation corruption is more discreet, "civilized" and genteel. The relationship between the first and second generation is similar to that between modern and traditional weaponry. "Uncivilized" corruption is like traditional weapons that shed blood before one's naked eyes whereas "civilized" corruption is like modern weapons in high-tech warfare where blinks on monitors hide all the cruelty of the battlefield and one tends to forget that modern weapons in fact often cause more devastation to human lives than traditional weapons.

Second-generation corruption has several features. First, its high level of deception. Wall Street manipulates financial leverage, packages derivative products and promotes various innovative combinations of "financial wizardry". Second, the American-style collusion of politicians and businessmen and power-for-money deals. A classic case may be the lobbying of congressmen by major corporations like Freddie Mac and Fannie Mae to gain advantages in revising the rules of the game. In turn, congressmen gain votes and political capital for their preferred housing policies. Third, large-scale regulatory arbitrage. Many dishonest acts were "selectively ignored" and many inferior financial products were given triple-A ratings by a few leading rating agencies and then sold to international investors, which caused worldwide havoc. Fourth, the use of legal loopholes and grey areas to gain exorbitant profits at the expense of public interests. How many people worldwide have been bankrupted by those irresponsible, fraudulent sales but have no recourse to recover their losses because they signed legally binding contracts that they did not understand (a case of "excessive legalism" and its damages). Fifth, the underlying philosophy of greed to "keep profits for oneself and leave costs to the society".

A study by Daniel Kaufmann of Brookings Institution on this kind of corruption reveals that if political contributions and lobbying are considered corruption, then the US is no longer a "low corruption" country and its level of corruption is ranked 53rd of the 102 countries surveyed.[2] And if financial corruption and its disastrous impact on the world were taken into account, US financial corruption would perhaps top the world. As a result, the median net worth of the American household fell by about 25% to around US$93,000, which is perhaps already lower than that of most families in China's developed regions.

All this seems to have caused declining public confidence in the American institutions. According to a General Social Survey by the University of Chicago, the percentage of Americans who have "a great deal of confidence" in American institutions, which was not high before, is continuously declining (Table 4.1).

Nobel laureate in economics Paul R. Krugman wrote in *The New York Times* on December 28, 2009, that "just about everyone in a policy-making position at the time believed in 1999 that America has honest corporate accounting; this lets investors make good decisions, and also forces management to behave responsibly; and the result is a stable, well-functioning

---

[2] Daniel Kaufmann, "Corruption and the Global Financial Crisis", *Forbes*, January 27, 2009.

Table 4.1   General Social Survey on the level of confidence of Americans in US institutions

	2000	2008
1. Great confidence in government	14%	11%
2. Great confidence in Congress	13%	11%
3. Great confidence in banks	30%	19%
4. Great confidence in corporations	30%	16%

Source: *The Economist*, March 28, 2009.

financial system. What percentage of all this turned out to be true? Zero." Krugman lamented that the self-deceiving, blind confidence was responsible for the US's "zero job creation, zero economic gains for the typical family, zero gains for stocks" in the past ten years.

In the mind of some Chinese scholars, the reform of the Chinese economy and political system means a transition to the American model, which is their ultimate point of reference. Yet, the current crisis and the general lack of trust in American public institutions within the US only show that the reform of the American system has a long way to go. No wonder even Francis Fukuyama, the author of *The End of History and the Last Man*, felt disappointed with the political decay in the US and published an op-ed article in the *Financial Times* on January 17, 2011 titled "US Democracy Has Little to Teach China". Some in China have lauded the American system and urged China to copy it, but how convincing is it if American trust in it is so low?

The Chinese system has its shortcomings but its reform has been continuous. Thanks to this unremitting effort, it is impossible to find a place within China's vast territory with a record of "zero job creation, zero economic gains for the typical family, zero gains for stocks" over the past three decades. But some scholars in China still refuse to acknowledge this fact and remain stubbornly obsessed with the American model. As an ancient Chinese saying goes, "Aim high to even get half". If you aim for the flawed American political and economic system, you will not even get half of it and will eventually lose all your own strong points. From this perspective, the Chinese economic and political reform should draw upon the strengths of others, go beyond the flawed American model, give full play to China's own strengths and promote more institutional innovations in line with China's local conditions.

4.2 The China Model May Win Out

In October 1987, János Kádár, General Secretary of the Hungarian Socialist Workers' Party, came to China and met with Deng Xiaoping. Early signs of turbulence in Eastern Europe and the Soviet Union were already visible and Deng Xiaoping counseled him not to imitate the West or other socialist countries and not to abandon the advantages of the socialist system.[3] It seemed that Kádár agreed with Deng but his colleagues back home thought otherwise and wanted to conduct a "thorough political reform" so as to turn Hungary into a "laboratory for democratic socialism". This led to the application of shock therapy in both the political and economic domains, i.e. a radical transformation from the original one-party structure into the Western-style multi-party system and from the original planned economy to a privatized market economy.

Twenty years have since passed, so what is the current situation in Hungary? According to a survey conducted by GfK, Germany's largest market research organization, in 2008, 62% of Hungarians felt their life today was worse than during the Kádár era; only 14% thought their life today was the happiest; while 60% felt life during the Kádár era was the happiest. I visited Hungary in 1989 and again 20 years later, and my field observations confirm these findings.

To my mind, Deng Xiaoping's counsel to Kádár has in fact highlighted the essence of the China model: do not imitate the West, do not imitate other socialist countries, and do not give up one's own advantages. On the basis of these "three noes," China has explored boldly various institutional innovations and drawn on others' strengths while giving play to its own strengths, gradually shaping its own model of development. In tackling the world financial crisis, China has demonstrated its ability for macro regulation, and the country was the first to emerge from the crisis. It is no wonder that George Soros, the Hungarian-American financier, claimed that China was the biggest beneficiary of globalization and the financial crisis. How did China become the biggest beneficiary? The main reason, I think, lies in its unique development model.

---

[3] Deng Xiaoping, *Deng Xiaoping Wenxuan* (Selected Works of Deng Xiaoping), Vol. 3, People's Press, Beijing, pp. 253–257.

This model has, inter alia, eight characteristics, namely, (1) practice-based reasoning, (2) a strong state, (3) prioritizing stability, (4) primacy of people's livelihood, (5) gradual reform, (6) correct priorities and sequence, (7) a mixed economy and (8) opening up to the outside world. This is also my summary of the experience of reform and opening up over the past three decades. These characteristics have taken shape on the basis of the Chinese civilizational state, especially the four aforementioned "super factors" of population, territory, tradition and culture. These "super factors" have largely determined the trajectory of China's development model. Over the past 30-odd years, some people have attempted to venture beyond these characteristics, but they are somehow compelled to return to them. This logic is perhaps determined by the innate genes of the Chinese civilizational state: China's development will suffer or even fail if it does not grow with its innate genes. Here are my brief explanations on the eight characteristics of the China model:

(1) *Practice-based Reasoning*

The philosophical outlook of the China model is based on practice. Guided by the motto of "seeking truth from facts", China proceeds from reality, rather than textbooks, and rejects any dogmatism. Drawing on its own as well as others' experiences, China has initiated bold yet prudent institutional reforms. This philosophical outlook is a product of the Chinese civilization, which possesses a strong this-worldly culture. Concerns about life, reality and society are always paramount in the Chinese world outlook. China does not have the theological tradition of the West, and its practice-based reasoning is part of China's secular cultural tradition.

Practice-based reasoning may be traced back to the "discourse on name and reality" (*mingshilun*) around 300 BC, i.e. "name" is to be verified by reality and "name" must match reality. Here, the "name" is not just a designation of an object, but all value judgments, and these judgments are to be verified by facts and reality. Chinese philosopher Zhao Tingyang presents this feature of the Chinese philosophical tradition in the following way: philosophers usually ask two questions: "to be", i.e. concerning "being" and "what is" in ontology, and "ought to be", i.e. concerning "what ought to be" in normative discourse, but the Chinese cultural tradition focuses more on practice and is more concerned with "to do" or "to do thus to be". In other words, it is a theory of practice based on doing, practicing and experimenting.[4]

The Chinese reformers are not content with ontology or normative theories of Western philosophy and place practice above them. The Chinese reformers do not accept lightly any Western abstract descriptions regarding questions like "What is the market economy?", "What should the market economy be like?", "What is democracy?" and "What should modernity be?" They engage in doing and experimenting in order to "investigate things" and then make their independent conclusions. In other words, the success of the China model is not dependent upon a deduction of value-based truths. Rather, the Chinese reformers place practice-based truths above value-based truths and initiate many pilot projects. Through repeated trials and errors, China has not only created an economic miracle but also redefined perhaps some truths that the West has taken for granted.

Perhaps due to this philosophical difference, reforms initiated by the West tend to start with constitutional amendments, followed by changes in laws and regulations and then implementation. The Chinese approach is just the opposite. China starts with experimentation and with pilot projects in small scale, and if successful, they are extended to other areas. This is then followed by changes in laws and regulations and ultimately constitutional amendments if need be. China on the whole adopts an inductive approach, rather than a deductive approach. Specifically, most Chinese are more inclined towards summarizing experiences and then producing theories. The Chinese hold that theories may help guide practice but practice may not always follow theories. In fact, the objective world has its own laws and one should be able to gradually uncover these laws through practice.

China does not accept political romanticism whereby reality must conform to certain theories. This is largely due to the fact that China has learnt useful lessons from its past experience of political romanticism. This logic of China's political culture has prevented the country from falling into, at least in the eyes of most Chinese today, political and economic "traps" such as shock therapy, wholesale privatization, financial crises and

---

[4] Zhao Tingyang, "智慧复兴的中国机会" (The Chinese Opportunity for a Renaissance of Wisdom), in 《学问中国》 (Ideas and Problems of China), Jiangxi Education Press, Nanchang, 1998, pp. 34–35.

paralyzing pseudo-democratization, and in the end China has ushered in its own spectacular rise.

(2) *A Strong State*

China has a relatively strong, disinterested and pro-development state, capable of setting out clear objectives for modernization and implementing development strategies and policies in the long-term interests of the country. The role of the state in China's economic development is in many ways determined by the aforementioned four "super factors" of population, territory, tradition and culture. China's centralized state started with the unification of the country by Emperor Qin Shihuang in 221 BC. The system of prefectures and counties (*junxianzhi*) was since established throughout the country. As a saying goes, "The Qin system has been inherited by all future dynasties." In this system, local officials were appointed by the central government, civil service exams were introduced during the Sui Dynasty around 600 AD, and officials were selected and appointed through *Keju* exams irrespective of their family backgrounds, contrary to the hereditary politics in European history, and the Chinese civil service was ahead of Europe's for well over 1,000 years. Europe later learnt from China the civil service examination system after the Enlightenment in the 18th century.

The sheer size of China adds complexity and challenges to its governance. Infrastructural demands, disaster relief and border defense all contributed to the evolution of a tradition in favor of a strong state, and this tradition is inseparable from the enormous challenges posed by governing a super-large and populous state, which is still the case today. Take for example the travel season of the annual Spring Festival over recent years, whereby the Chinese return home for family reunions during the Festival—itself evidence of the Chinese cultural tradition. More than 2 billion trips are made each year. The Spring Festival of 2011 saw 2.9 billion trips. What does 2.9 billion trips mean? Imagine the total population of North and South America, Europe and Africa moving from one place to another within a month. No other political system can cope with that kind of challenge, except for a highly efficient state like China.

In the past three decades of reform and opening up, the state power forged in China's long history and the party power formed in the tumultuous revolutions and development have all been used to promote China's modernization as well as reform initiatives. A major issue with all those developing countries that adopt the Western model is what Nobel laureate Karl Gunnar Myrdal termed the "soft state". A "soft state" is weak in its powers of execution, as governments of these countries are forever hijacked by various vested interests, and by politicians' perpetual bickering and infighting. They can hardly reach a consensus on building a bridge or a highway, not to mention implementing family planning policies or surpassing the developed countries. As a result, their modernization stagnates, and there is no chance whatsoever for them to catch up with the developed world, not to mention surpassing it.

China has accomplished the largest industrial and social revolutions in human history over the past three decades and lifted over 400 million people out of poverty. This process is accompanied by social tensions and dislocations of all kinds, but a relatively strong, disinterested and diligent state has successfully prevented China from losing control or falling into chaos as is the case with some other countries, and has effectively reduced possible social conflicts associated with large-scale social transformations. State intervention and persuasion have lowered the costs of resolving various social conflicts. The Chinese state has arguably the most efficient organizational power in the world as evident in China's hosting of the Olympic Games in Beijing in 2008 and the World Expo in Shanghai in 2010 and in tackling the financial crisis since 2008. This competence of the state is crucial for China's march towards a first-rate developed nation.

In terms of governance, the Chinese state is naturally also faced with the task of its own reforms and institutional innovations in such areas as how to readjust the relations between state and enterprises, and between state and society, and how to ensure effective supervision of the state. In the field of economic development, the state should have a clearer delineation of the scope of its intervention. Yet in the Chinese political culture, any weakening or transformation of the state functions is usually initiated by the state itself, as has been the case in China's reform process where Beijing has introduced a good many initiatives for large-scale decentralization in the decision-making process.

(3) *Prioritizing Stability*

China has on the whole maintained a good balance between stability, reform and development over the past three decades. With a huge population and limited resources, competition for scarce resources in a country like China can lead easily to instability. Moreover, the legacy of "hundreds of states in one" also implies that China has far more cultural and ethnic diversity than most other countries, and such diversity has often been the cause of clashes and conflicts throughout China's long history. China's stability is also threatened by separatist and hostile forces. Some in the West still hope for the independence of Tibet, Xinjiang, Taiwan and Inner Mongolia, and even expect a kind of breakup of China the way the former Soviet Union and ex-Yugoslavia did. But these attempts stand little chance to succeed thanks to the mainstream Chinese tradition in favor of a strong and unified state, to the general inclination of most Chinese for a united prosperous country and to China's rapid emergence as the world's largest single market.

The sheer scale of the Chinese civilizational state also means that there are more causes of domestic instability in China than most other countries, which could be hugely destructive. This is why Deng Xiaoping, the architect of China's reform and opening up, repeatedly stated, "Stability (in China) prevails over everything else," and observed, "Of all the issues China is faced with, ensuring stability is paramount. Without an environment of stability, nothing can be achieved, and whatever gains we have made could be lost easily." During his 1992 inspection tour of southern China, he stressed the same point that "History does not provide China many opportunities for development, and a country could collapse overnight (if things go wrong). It is easy to destroy but difficult to build up the nation," and "If chaos occurs, it will be very difficult (for China) to recover in many years to come." This is Deng's sober conclusion based on his reading of the history of China and the world and his personal political experience.

I myself have made a rough calculation: in the 140 years from the Opium War in 1839 to the reform and opening up in 1978, the longest period of stability in China was no more than eight or nine years. Peasant uprisings, foreign invasions, warlords fighting each other, civil wars, political movements one after another disrupted China's peace and economic development and caused untold suffering to the people. Finally, Deng, China's paramount leader, made up his mind to take a firm stand on ensuring China's political stability in order to improve people's living standards, and China has finally achieved three decades of sustained development unprecedented in China's modern history. Indeed, the key to the success of the China model is to promote reform and opening up and economic development in a stable environment in this vast and populous country.

In turn, the civilizational state has its own political logic and tradition and its legacy of *taiping shengshi* (great prosperity in overall peace). So long as the state maintains stability and peace and pursues an enlightened policy for development, most Chinese will work hard and prosper, as under peace, most Chinese are able to display their tradition of "diligence creating wealth", which is the case with all Chinese communities throughout the world. Obstacles and problems can be overcome in the process of development so long as China is stable and keeps its pace of development. But it is necessary to mention that prioritizing stability does not mean evading challenges or problems. On the contrary, stability creates favorable conditions for more effective solutions to many challenges.

(4) *Primacy of People's Livelihood*

China has a tradition of having a people-oriented economy for thousands of years, hence the ancient saying that "The people are the foundation of the state, and when the foundation is stable, the country is peaceful." In this context, people's livelihood was viewed with great importance as something capable of determining the fate of the country. In the old age of the subsistence economy, the Chinese state was keenly aware of the golden rule which dictates that "Food is the staff of life". This tradition has continued to this day, as ensuring enough food and other daily necessities for the vast population has always been of paramount concern to China's top leadership till this day. The various goals put forward in the course of reform such as "Having enough to eat and wear for the people" and "Achieving moderate prosperity for all" embody the Chinese tradition of prioritizing people's livelihood.

The Chinese experience since 1978 shows that a developing country must take the improvement of people's standard of living as its top priority, and regard poverty eradication as a core human right, as poverty, especially abject poverty, undermines basic human dignity and rights. With this belief, China has done its utmost to improve people's standard of living and achieved remarkable results in poverty eradication. The statistics of the United Nations shows that nearly 70% of the world's poverty eradication has occurred in China over the past two decades.

Today, approximately half of the world's population still lives in poverty. The Western model has failed to solve the basic problem of people's livelihood in the developing world, and so much manpower and financial resources have been diverted by self-serving politicians who in the name of promoting "democratization" engage themselves in power rivalry, which more often than not ends in constant chaos with "elephants fighting each other while the grass suffers", i.e. politicians fighting each other for their own interests while ordinary people suffer.

From this perspective, even in terms of promoting political reform in China, one should still focus on improving the quality of people's lives in all aspects. Political reform should not be separated from improving people's livelihood. Furthermore, higher living standards create the necessary conditions conducive to political reform. The reform must ultimately provide good governance to ensure that people live a safer, freer, happier and more dignified life. Democratization in many non-Western countries, as designed after the Western model, is often for the sake of democratization, rather than for tangible benefits for the people, and such efforts often have no bearing whatsoever on improving livelihood, leading, not infrequently, to ethnic and religious conflicts and even wars.

Experience has shown that if a developing country cannot establish a broad domestic consensus on giving top priority to improving people's standard of living, and if it places its hope for solving all its domestic problems on radical political reform, its chance of success is perhaps zero. Radical political reforms tend to create high expectations among the people and lead to explosive political participation and economic chaos, and eventually greater disillusionment among the people. If this kind of radical approach cannot even succeed in a country like Mongolia with a population of less than 3 million or Kyrgyzstan with a population of less than 6 million, how can it work for a huge country like China with a population of 1.3 billion?

(5) *Gradual Reform*

In a vast, populous and diverse country like China, top-level decision-makers are always faced with the enormous challenge of insufficient information. This implies greater risks in policy-making for decision-makers, and it is only reasonable for them to lean towards gradual reform whereby they can lower the risks of reform and make sure that all possible negative effects of their policy initiatives are under control. As a result, Beijing tends to encourage various local experiments throughout the reform process, and then extend elsewhere whatever is successful in the experiments. Deng used the ancient Chinese proverb of "Crossing the river by feeling for stepping stones" to describe this trial-and-error approach to China's reform.

Moreover, thanks to the size of its territory and population, China had never achieved a fully planned economy as with the Soviet Union and Eastern Europe. Consequently, China perhaps had better initial conditions for market-oriented reforms than the Soviet Union and Eastern Europe, as even at the high time of the planned economy, there were still scattered private economic activities in different parts of the country. With the loosening of policies as reform progressed, the market has grown more spontaneously and vigorously than in Russia and Eastern Europe. Beijing has observed carefully many bottom-up spontaneous reform initiatives and eventually approved and extended them across the country as part of its overall strategy for reform and opening up.

Gradual reform is different from radical reform or what is called shock therapy. Radical reform is based on the ideal of the Western political model, including pluralistic politics and popular democracy, which simply dismantles the original political order and replaces it with a new one. In contrast, gradual reform is premised on the stability of the existing political order and continuation of China's relatively strong state. China has categorically rejected shock therapy and promoted gradual and constant reform. Rather than abandoning the existing imperfect system, it has made use of the system as far as possible to serve the purpose of modernization while reforming it gradually. Reform does not require perfection but entails steady progress and constant corrections, and the objective of the reform is reached through the accumulation of many gradual reform initiatives. This has proved to be an effective way to achieve success.

Furthermore, gradualism does not necessarily mean slow change all the time. On the contrary, while China's overall strategy for reform is gradual, its actual execution is often highly efficient. For example, China's opening up started with the establishment of four special economic zones in southern China, and this was gradual in terms of China's overall strategy for opening up, but its execution was efficient with four zones established and operating well soon after the relevant decision has been adopted, demonstrating the kind of efficiency associated with the country's rapid transformation.

(6) *Correct Priorities and Sequence*

In line with gradualism, China has established the right priorities and sequence for change. The reform is not expected to be completed in one go, and a series of priorities in reform have taken shape in the course of reform. The reform and opening up over the past 30 years have shown a broad pattern of change: easy reforms first, difficult ones second. Reform usually starts first in the relatively low-cost areas that entail better pay-offs, hence resistance is lower and pay-offs are higher. Then efforts are made to reform the existing institutions. For example, China's reform started with agriculture, which was the relatively easy part of the overall reform.

The reform of state-owned enterprises (SOEs) also began first with the expansion of decision-making power and profit retention. As a result, there were more beneficiaries than losers in the reform process. This approach to reform creates suitable conditions, accumulates experience, reduces resistance and tends to bring about chain reactions for other reforms. For instance, the successful rural reform provided a huge market and adequate labor supply for the subsequent urban reform. Private enterprises were started from scratch and multiplied and in turn created a competitive environment for the market economy and laid the groundwork for reforming state-owned enterprises.

Having the correct priorities and sequence is inseparable from China's holistic and dialectic philosophical traditions. The Chinese hold that it is necessary to approach all issues from a holistic perspective, rather than merely a partial treatment. This has allowed Beijing to make better strategic decisions and handle issues with the right priorities and in the right sequence. The reform and opening up over the past three decades have proceeded in a clear sequence: rural reform first, urban reform second; reform in the coastal areas first, the hinterland second; economic reform first, political reform second. Most reform initiatives are not conceived to be completed in one go. Rather, "two steps forward, one step back" is often the norm. However, reform has been continuous and completed through a step-by-step approach and the accumulation of many reform initiatives. This process seems to be one befitting China's status as a civilizational state with its super-large population, vast territory, diverse traditions and rich cultures.

(7) *Mixed Economy*

China's present economic system is called a socialist market economy, which is essentially a mixed economy, a mixture of the "invisible hand" and the "visible hand", an amalgamation of market forces and state power, and a fusion of the principles of market economics and humanistic economics.

China largely established the socialist market economic system over the past three decades, and the system has, in relative terms, the efficiency of resource allocation in a market economy and the capacity for macro regulation in a socialist economy. China is rightly suspicious of market fundamentalism in part due to its historical traditions. For instance, Beijing has all along rejected the call for land privatization, a tenet of orthodox market economics, as "All land under heaven belongs to the emperor" is part of the Chinese tradition, while the ideal of revolutionaries throughout Chinese history is "Land to the tiller". It is widely held in China that as a country with a large population and low per capita arable land, privatization of land may easily lead to polarization, whereby land will be concentrated in the hands of a few and many farmers will lose land and fall into poverty.

Instead of imitating the Western model of private land ownership, China has shown ingenuity in separating the right of land ownership from that of land use, and created, to the amazement of many, the world's largest property market, urbanization process and high-speed rail network, the world's second-largest network of expressways, and a home ownership rate higher than that of the developed countries.

As it is moving ahead with the objective of building a society of "moderate prosperity", China has increasingly integrated itself with the world economy. In this process, China has learnt what can be called "numerical management" from the West, but has also developed its unique capacity for macro regulation on the basis of state ownership of land, major financial institutions and large state-owned enterprises. The Chinese state has demonstrated its capacity to plan and execute key national projects and promote the fast expansion of the private sector.

Over the past three decades, the central government has provided strategic guidance for the country's overall changes and ensured macro stability for the nation, while the local governments at all levels, especially at the county level, utilize taxation, land and other policies to attract investment and promote local employment and prosperity. The fact that both the central and the local governments are the engines driving the Chinese economy explains to a great extent China's miracle.

This kind of interaction between the central and local governments in promoting the economy has a long history in China and can be traced back to the prefectural and county system of the Qin and Han dynasties 2,000 years ago, to the Wang Anshi reform of the Song Dynasty (AD 960–1279) and his policy of "vertical control" of counties, to his contemporary Sima Guang's idea of interactions between local governments and local gentry and to Chairman Mao Zedong's policy of "walking on two legs".

As a civilizational state, the size of a Chinese province is often equal to four or five medium-sized European states, and China naturally has the world's largest network of local governments, and it is essential for Beijing to bring into play the initiatives of China's local governments for development while maintaining the country's overall political and economic stability. Economist Steven N. S. Cheung (Zhang Wuchang) argues that the biggest secret behind China's miracle is the competition among local governments, especially competition at the county level, as the county government decides on the use of the land. "A formidable economic force has been created [through] an expansion of contract responsibility system between local government institutions and private enterprises."[5]

Economist Shi Zhengfu holds that the success of the Chinese economic reform is largely due to the dynamic interactions between the three parties (central leadership, various ministries and local governments). He argues that in the former Soviet Union and Eastern Europe, there were only two parties (central leadership and various ministries), and failures became inevitable as ministries tended to resist reform initiatives from the top leaders so as to protect their own vested interests. In contrast, local governments in China are participants and have a stake in the success of China's economic reform, thus breaking the reform stalemate characteristic of the dual-party structure of Russia and Eastern Europe.[6]

Naturally, the tri-party structure is not perfect, and issues of "rent-seeking" and local protectionism still exist. Yet it is still more positive than negative for China's economic development, and it is necessary to acknowledge this and then strive to improve the work of the government. It is unwise to underestimate China's own success as a way to fit Western economics textbooks or political science literature. Rather, what we should do is to base ourselves on the successful Chinese experience and revise these books or write our own textbooks. The Chinese experience has proven that the role played by various levels of the Chinese government is part of China's core competitiveness in the world today, and naturally, it is also true that the role of the government is by no means perfect, and the role and functions of different levels of government in China should be more clearly delineated and their various weaknesses can be and should be overcome in the future.

To my mind, if a civilizational state like China is to function well, it needs apparently something beyond market economics, beyond multiplying business transactions, beyond individual or group interests, something

---

[5] Steven N. Cheung, 《中国的经济制度》 (The Economic System of China), Zhongxin Press, 2009.

[6] Shi Zhengfu, "史无前例30年：中国发展道路的政治经济学" (Unprecedented 30 Years: The Political Economy of China's Development Path), in Shi Zhengfu (ed.), 《30年与60年：中国的改革与发展》 (30 Years and 60 Years: China's Reform and Development), Shanghai People's Press, Shanghai, 2009, pp. 1–24.

capable of bringing into play the initiatives of all the parties and achieving the unique Chinese-style objective of "satisfying the demands of the people". This "something" is probably none other than the holistic and strategic thinking of the Chinese tradition as well as a strong and disinterested state that understands the public sentiment and people's overall interests. If a civilizational state or the China model does not have all this, the prospects for China's economic and political development can hardly be optimistic, and China may eventually become a loser in this world of fierce economic and political competition.

(8) *Opening Up to the Outside World*

In terms of historical traditions, China was a fairly open country from its first unification during the Qin Dynasty in 221 BC to the famous overseas voyages led by Admiral Zheng He in the Ming Dynasty during the early 15th century. Openness and exchanges between nations had greatly enriched the Chinese civilization and helped spread it around the world. However, the Ming emperors later shifted away from openness and adopted a policy of self-seclusion and imposed a maritime ban following Admiral Zheng He's grand voyages. In retrospect, if China had remained open to the outside world, it would have either produced its own industrial revolution or embraced the British one, and then world history would have been totally different.

Deng Xiaoping's strategy of comprehensive opening up has reconnected China with the outside world, and this opening-up policy has been pursued with a step-by-step approach: first, opening up the coastal areas, followed by opening up the areas along the major rivers and Chinese border areas, and finally opening up the whole hinterland. During the Cold War era, the US had intentionally excluded the former Soviet bloc from the US-led world market. In retrospect, Stalin's introduction of "dual-world-market system" (the socialist market system vs. the capitalist market system) was perhaps just what the Americans wanted. Deng's strategy was different. As he believed that isolationism was the major cause of China's decline in modern history, he promoted China's comprehensive opening up and integration with the global market as well as its participation in international competition. He urged the country to adapt itself to such competition and try to learn whatever was good from others but to do so selectively, rather than blindly following others.

The confidence behind this policy of extensive opening up originates from China's past history, as the country was prosperous when it was more open to the outside world, as the case with the most prosperous dynasty, the Tang Dynasty (AD 618–907). The Chinese civilization seems to have a remarkable capacity to maintain its vigor and constantly rejuvenize itself so long as it is open to the outside world. This was the case in the past, remains so at present and will be so in the future. China's opening up, as before, has energized all the essential elements of the Chinese civilization and reinvigorated China as a nation through its extensive engagements with the outside world, through learning from others selectively, cultural borrowing and open competition. Meanwhile, opening up also allows China to understand the outside world more objectively, including all the strengths and weaknesses of other countries and their political and economic systems, and thus build up China's own confidence that the Chinese experience and wisdom can be useful to all of humanity.

The China model is indeed attractive to much of the world today. China has been growing fast both in good times and bad times. Vladimir Popov, a Russian economist, commented in September 2006 that "China's development model is irresistibly attractive to the developing countries because it accounts for a rapid growth unprecedented in world economic history. This model runs contrary to the US-advocated Western democracy or neo-liberalism." President Abdoulaye Wade of Senegal observed, "Despite the Western countries' complaint about China's slow pace in adopting democratic reforms, it cannot conceal the fact that the Chinese are more competitive, more efficient and more adaptive in businesses in Africa than their Western critics. Not just Africa but the West itself has much to learn from China." Lawrence Summers, former US Treasury Secretary, also said, "In two or three centuries from now, historians will find that the 9/11 and the Iraq War are largely insignificant, and the rise of China may well be the sole important event in the 21st century."

Certainly, China must remain vigilant. Even though the China model seems to work well and has scored enormous successes, this model is still imperfect and evolving. And some of the problems faced by the model are serious and call for earnest solutions. For example, excessive government intervention in certain areas has created a deficient market; insufficient political reform in certain sectors has caused monopolies and rent-seeking corruption; the gap between rich and poor, problems in ecology, education, healthcare, etc., have all caused much discontent within the country. However, so long as we are clear-headed, determined and resourceful, these problems can be resolved eventually, and this process may in fact create new opportunities for China's further development, as an important lesson gained from China's reform over the past three decades is to treat all problems as opportunities for more and better development.

In some sense, one may also claim that the China model is "the least bad" model. That is to say, although the model has its flaws, some of which are even serious, it is still better than the models employed by other developing or transitional countries, especially when comparing China's success in the past 30 years with those countries that have applied the West-directed development models. For instance, the Structural Adjustment Programs imposed by the IMF on Africa during the 1980s and 1990s reduced sharply public expenditures and finally caused the worsening of Africa's economic and social crises. The shock therapy promoted by the US in Russia is now widely viewed by the Russians as the "third catastrophe" (the earlier ones being the Mongol invasion in the 14th century and the Nazi invasion during the Second World War). The Washington consensus compelled the developing countries to promote liberalization of their capital markets regardless of their national conditions, which was a major cause of the 1997 Asian financial crisis and the Argentine economic crisis. These crises often led to a rollback of decades of development for the victim countries, and market fundamentalism, to my mind, is also responsible for the current financial crash originating in the US.

In hindsight, it is perhaps reasonable to say that if China had followed blindly the Western model or failed to adhere to its own path of development, the country may have already experienced huge chaos and even a breakup. China has largely succeeded in exploring its own path of modernization over the past 30 years. With a population greater than the total population of the European Union, the US, Japan and Russia, China has undergone its own industrial, technological and social revolutions while maintaining its overall stability, improved drastically the living standards of the vast majority of its population and avoided the 1997 and 2008 financial crises. It would already be remarkable for any country to attain any one of these achievements, but China has achieved all of them, and this fact alone is a proof of the success of the China model.

The China model has taken shape amidst large-scale international interactions and competition and it is hence dynamic and competitive. The specific methods employed in this model may not necessarily be applicable to other countries, but its inherent ideas such as "seeking truth from facts", "primacy of people's livelihood", "harmonious development", "trial-and-error gradualism" and "holistic thinking," may well inspire many other countries and people in the world, and these ideas may go a long way in helping to resolve some acute and pressing issues of global governance. I will discuss this point further in the next chapter.

4.3 Shaping the Chinese Standards

Riding the Shinkansen during his visit to Japan in October 1978, Deng Xiaoping personally experienced Japan's bullet train and told the reporters with him then, "This is like pushing us to run, and we need very much to run." Deng was referring to China's pressing need for speedy modernization. If he were still alive, Deng would be most pleased to know that China has been "running" and "racing against time" over the past three decades in order to catch up with the developed countries. While the Shinkansen is still operating at 250 km/h since Deng's last ride 32 years ago, China has developed its own high-speed rail with a top operational speed at 394 km/h. The total length of the Chinese high-speed railway has also overtaken that of Europe and Japan. In his State of the Union address in 2010, President Obama noted, "There is no reason why China should have the fastest trains," and he apparently wanted to inspire his countrymen to work harder, with the example of China's rapid rise as shown in high-speed rail.

The history of modernization seems to be marked by change in speed, which is often a symbol of progress in modernization and rising living standards. Western historians often describe the period from 1848 to 1875 as the times of "economic revolution", when speed was increasingly accelerated. During that period, iron and steel output increased sharply; railways spanned Europe and North America; the Suez Canal was opened;

many new cities emerged; millions of migrants moved everywhere; the Industrial Revolution peaked in Britain and waves of industrial revolutions swept the US, France and Germany; and the West established its leadership in the world.

Today, Chinese high-speed rail is driving the largest scale of urbanization in human history, with planned high-speed railways linking China's three world-class economic rings (the Yangtze River Delta around Shanghai, the Pearl River Delta around Guangzhou-Shenzhen-Hong Kong, and the Beijing-Tianjin metropolis) and reducing the traveling time between Beijing and Shanghai from over ten hours to less than five hours and uniting half of China's 1.3 billion population through the world's largest high-speed grid composed of four north-south corridor lines and four east-west corridor lines. It is not only changing the speed of rail travel but also transforming people's concept of time and space. It is creating the world's largest unified market, which also signifies the rise of the Chinese standards in modernization.

This endeavor is by no means easy and bound to encounter difficulties and challenges, and there was even a tragic accident involving a collision between two second-tier D-type trains (at 200–250 km/h) in the spring of 2011 near the city of Wenzhou, causing a death toll of 40 passengers, but this accident occurred after the D-type trains had been in safe operation for four years, carrying over 700 million passengers. The sad event will enable China to pursue its set objectives more prudently in the future and will in no way decrease the significance of China's rapid progress in high-speed rail and other related industries.

What is more interesting, to this author, is the Chinese approach towards developing the Chinese standards in high-speed rail, which can be summarized as follows: China attracts foreign investors with its huge domestic market, and negotiates with them to transfer part of their technologies. China then organizes more than 100,000 researchers and engineers to study and digest the imported technologies, and works on this basis to innovate and then develop China's own technological standards which are higher than the imported ones. In a broader context, this approach also reflects the overall strategic thinking behind the China model of development, i.e. to learn from the strengths of others, while also giving play to China's own strengths, and it is on this basis that

China strives to go beyond the Western standards and shape its own standards.

The story of Tian Ji in horse racing which I have mentioned earlier also applies here. As the developed countries are ahead of China in many areas, how can China catch up and eventually surpass them? China has adopted Tian Ji's strategy, i.e. in a situation where your overall strength is weaker, you should be aware of and make the best use of your comparative advantages, and create and build up your own asymmetric strengths over your opponents and eventually win. This is what China has done with regard to shaping its own standards in high-speed rail development, and broadly speaking, this is also a strategy of making innovations and creating new standards on the basis of combining one's own strengths and those of others. This philosophy has in fact underpinned many of China's reform initiatives since 1978:

China has learnt a lot from the Western market economy to promote China's market economy, which ensures greater efficiency in resource allocation, but it has also drawn on its own tradition of a strong state and eventually created the innovative socialist market economy. The Chinese economic system has thus endeavored to combine the efficiency of the market economy and the strength of overall balance of socialism, which, to a large extent, accounts for China's sustained growth for more than three decades.

China has drawn on the Western "numeral management" to improve its management in all aspects of the economy, but it has also developed its own capacity for macro regulation. China's policy for macro regulation is pursued both in good and bad economic times. This is to a great extent the reason why Beijing succeeded in avoiding the 1997 Asian financial crisis and the 2008 financial crash.

China has learnt from the US to increase its economic competitiveness, but it has avoided what many perceive as excessive capitalism in the American system. China has learnt from Europe's many welfare initiatives, but it has avoided the European-style excessive welfare state. China is still exploring its own way forward, but its guiding philosophy is clear, i.e. to create an economic and social development model that is, to the extent possible efficient and fair, while avoiding the pitfalls of the American or the Greek model.

China has learnt from the Western businesses in promoting the rapid expansion of its private sector but it has also conducted wide-ranging reform of the state-owned enterprises, particularly in terms of redefining property rights and clarifying various responsibilities. The state and private sectors play their separate functions and are expected to be complementary to each other. Despite the occasional tensions between them, China's overall strategy is not "more state sector and less private sector" or vice versa, but "stronger state sector and stronger private enterprises". Both sectors are expected to do better and complement each other, which in turn drive China's economy as a whole. This strategy may not yet be fully realized, but its objective is clear and, to my mind, achievable.

China has learnt from the West in reshaping its legal system and established almost from scratch a rather comprehensive legal framework for practicing the rule of law in the country, but it has also tapped into China's political and legal resources to establish a series of characteristically Chinese politico-legal institutions such as large-scale social mediations, reconciliations and "comprehensive management" (*zonghezhili*). Although there are still challenges in building a society based on the rule of law, China is clear about its general orientation in this endeavor, i.e. continuous promotion of the rule of law, yet avoiding the excessive legalism of the West, with the aim of building a new type of legal regime, which is fairer, more effective and less costly than the Western one.

China has learnt from the West in greatly expanding individual rights and freedoms, but it has continued its tradition of focusing on family harmony and collective rights. Hence, the current Chinese society is more dynamic and coherent than the Western one, without losing the central role of the family and national unity. The combination of Chinese and Western cultures and approaches has helped China overcome many challenges that baffle many other countries.

In brief, the philosophy behind the China model is to return to the Chinese tradition of synthesizing and innovating, practice-based reasoning, and "midstream living" and the Confucian school of the golden mean. With this approach, China's probability of success is higher. China is still faced with many challenges, but having the correct strategy means the job is perhaps already half done.

I should also mention briefly here the debate within China on the merits of railways vs. expressways a few years back. Some had argued that with the advent of cars, so long as there was a well-connected network of expressways, the first choice of travel for the general public would be expressways, whereas the use of railways would steadily decline, as cars can secure door-to-door travel and are more convenient than trains. They also cited the experiences of the developed countries like the US and the UK, where rail transportation steadily declined. Why, then, would China not prioritize the construction of expressways? Local governments were also enthusiastic about expressway construction as it was easier to attract investment for real estate development along expressways and thus boost the local economies.

By now, China has completed a network of expressways spanning the whole country after ten years of continuous construction and it has brought about a highly positive impact on the Chinese economy and social life. Yet, at the same time, the railways have not declined. On the contrary, China has embraced a new round of rapid railway development, and by 2020, a network of high-speed rail for the whole country is expected to be completed. I recall the expressway-railway debate here to make a point that the issues in China must be resolved in ways that suit the Chinese conditions. China's population is four times that of the US, and the number of people traveling during the annual Spring Festival is greater than the total population of North and South America, Europe and Africa. Therefore, the model of cars and expressways works for the US but not for a huge and populous country like China. The development of China's transportation system must include a whole range of different models.

The relative success of China's high-speed rail also highlights the fact that if certain standards are created in China, they will generate an international impact. Fundamentally speaking, competition in the field of setting standards is the fiercest in the world, and this is true in the economic and technological field, and also true in the political domain. There are three strategies in the global competition of standards. The first one is to be a follower, i.e. to use standards set by others, and this is the lowest in value creation. The second is to be a participant, i.e. to participate in setting international standards, and this is better than the first strategy. The third is to be a leader, i.e. to lead the competition in setting international standards and have others follow your standards. This represents the highest value creation.

One of the major characteristics of a civilizational state is its innate ability to create standards. The West has always adopted the leadership strategy in setting international political standards and promoting Western political values globally to serve its strategic interests. With the normative power of their political narratives, some Western countries do not even bother to make apologies when they have created havoc and impoverished other countries as in the case of the devastating Iraq War, where the war was projected as promoting so-called "universal values".

In the field of setting international political standards, China should adopt the leadership or participation strategy or both, and this is what we have learnt from the relative success of China's high-speed rail and other initiatives such as hosting the Olympic Games, reforming the state sector and preventing the financial crises in China. The next decade is crucial for China in terms of creating the Chinese standards as the country is well on its way to becoming the world's largest economy.

CHAPTER 5

THE RISE OF A NEW POLITICAL DISCOURSE

5.1 Political Reform, the Chinese Way

The Chinese experience since 1978 is often described in the Western media as "economic reform without political reform". Yet any significant change of the Soviet-type system, as has been the case with China, inevitably entails a considerable reform of its political and administrative system. In this context, the Chinese experience may better be described as "great economic reform with lesser political reform".

The significance of China's economic reform not only lies in the rapidly expanding economy and greatly improved living standards of most of the Chinese, but also in its profound implications for China's social and political life. Institutions underpinning the rigid state control prior to 1978 have either disappeared or substantially weakened: with the rising prosperity, the rationing system for consumer goods disappeared, and the old rationing coupons are now collector's items; with growing social mobility, the household registration (*hukou*) and personnel dossier (*dang-an*) systems have drastically loosened up; and most people are no longer dependent for their livelihoods on the state or work units (*danwei*), as most of the wealth and jobs in China today are generated outside the state sector. China's economic reform has not only brought about greater prosperity for the country, but also created unprecedented opportunities for the Chinese to pursue their own interests and shape their own destinies. The average Chinese today has far more freedom of personal choice than anytime since 1949. Individuals can make their own choice regarding jobs, housing, education, marriage and leisure, and can move freely within the country or travel abroad for leisure, study or work. This marks a monumental change from the old era of a shortage economy and extremely tight political control, and all these changes are inseparable from many "lesser political reforms" adopted since 1978, which include the following:

First, mass ideological campaigns based on the radical doctrine of class struggle were repudiated so that people could pursue normal lives and material interests.

Second, virtually all political victims from the preceding periods, numbering tens of millions, were rehabilitated, including many professionals whose skills were indispensable for China's modernization.

Third, across China's vast countryside, the people's commune was abolished, thus ending this rigid system of political, economic and administrative control that had impoverished Chinese peasants.

Fourth, village-level elections have been carried out in the Chinese countryside, as a massive political experiment to introduce rudimentary democracy. This practice is now being introduced into some cities as pilot projects for neighborhood-level elections.

Fifth, there are other political reform experiments, such as the cadre rotation system to break *guanxi* (personal connection) networks, as well as the practice of a "small government and big society", which downsizes bureaucracy and forsakes its many functions that can be better performed by society, and therefore urges governments to facilitate, not micromanage, the operation of a market economy.

Sixth, the mandatory retirement system has been introduced throughout the bureaucratic structure from the top leadership down to the grassroots workplace. China's top leadership serves a maximum of two terms for a total of ten years.

Seventh, think tanks have popped up across the country to provide advice to decision-makers, especially at the national and provincial levels.

Eighth, an extensive experiment and practice of "selection" plus some form of "election" are introduced into the appointment and promotion of cadres at all levels.

Ninth, in the broad context of political reform, various initiatives have facilitated unprecedented social mobility, more diversified values, more elastic ideological standards, many steps to curb the administrative power of the state over the economy and the society, more laws and legal institutions, the energizing of people's congresses, and the drastic relaxing of cultural restrictions.

China's political reforms are essentially attempts at political rationalization, not Western-style democratization, aimed at facilitating rapid economic and social development and improving the efficiency of the existing political system and people's living standards. In contrast to the radical model of democratization, which involves an uncompromising break with the past, Chinese reformers have carried out those "lesser political reforms" by working through existing political institutions.

The Chinese approach to political reform has produced generally positive results. In particular, China has ensured sustained political stability for its economic development and vastly improved living standards for its people for over three decades. Furthermore, this cautious approach has enabled the country to avert the possible economic and social upheavals which could have resulted from rushing too fast into a radically different economic and political system, as witnessed in the former Soviet Union and ex-Yugoslavia, where radical political change led to economic meltdown and political breakup.

China's priority of economic reform has in fact determined the scope of China's political reform, i.e. removing immediate political obstacles to China's economic and social progress. This approach is on the whole responsive to the pressing needs of most Chinese for developing the economy and improving their living standards. This approach is a disappointment for many pro-West intellectuals in China, but it has indeed provided ordinary people with unprecedented freedoms and contributed to China's fast re-emergence in the world.

Chinese reformers have shown their ability to ensure long-term policy coherence and macro political and economic stability, through a combination of administrative and market methods. A significant portion of the party/state structure has developed its competence and expertise in shaping and implementing various reform initiatives. For instance, a dense web of local compliance mechanisms has been established to facilitate the execution of reform policies, ranging from attracting foreign investment to setting up development zones. Policy enforcement for common goals has been on the whole effective, as shown in the reform of the state-owned enterprises and Chinese banking sector, in the high absorptive capacity for foreign direct investments, in the state's capacity to build a first-rate infrastructure and in the fight against the financial crisis in 2008.

China is still going through its own industrial and technological revolutions, and continued political shifts and social dislocations are inevitable. The increasing gap between regions, unemployment, corruption, massive internal migration, and the gap between rich and poor are all issues calling for more economic, social and political reforms.

A number of new measures have been adopted by China's top leadership over the past few years: emphasis on promoting the rule of law and staying close to the masses; the Political Bureau reporting annually to the full Central Committee; more attention and assistance to the poorer regions and vulnerable social groups; revision of the Constitution by including clauses for protecting human rights and private property; greater room for the media and the Internet to reflect public opinion; the idea of a "political civilization" with more emphasis on procedures; a system of independent commissioners to supervise provincial cadres; and more comprehensive accountability at various levels of government to people and people's congresses.

The transformation of the Chinese state will continue, driven by China's economic reform, social change and integration with the outside world. But China's political transition is likely to continue its present cautious approach and its top-down and gradual process. The party's "zone of indifference" will further expand in the years to come, while tolerance for radical dissent may remain limited. And China's successful economic reform may well set a pattern for China's political reform. The political consensus in China today is still on a syncretic approach, drawing on whatever is good from the outside while gradually reforming China's political system. Most Chinese reformers believe that political reform should be a gradual, pragmatic and experimental process much like the experience of economic reform, and that a strong state remains a crucial prerequisite for ensuring macroeconomic and political stability amidst the multiplying economic and social challenges.

The Russian experience suggests that it is by no means easy to create a viable political system in place of the old regime in a large country with no tradition of Western-style democracy and adversarial politics. Furthermore, as far as China is concerned, after more than a century of devastating wars and chaotic revolutions, and after three decades of successful economic reform, most Chinese seem to be more willing to embrace gradual reform than radical revolution.

My own counsel on China's political reform is essentially to follow three principles: First, it should continue to be a gradual reform. It is unrealistic to design a perfect master plan, and political romanticism is highly dangerous for a civilizational state like China characterized by "hundreds of states in one". Beijing should take into consideration the actual conditions of the country, proceed step by step, conduct experiments and encourage people to make innovations. As long as China pursues this approach based on the idea of "crossing the river by feeling for stepping stones", China, as with its successful economic reform, will always find the right stones and finally cross the river, meaning that China will eventually shape a new type of democratic system.

Like with its economic reform, while China does not have a roadmap, it has a "compass". The broad orientation of the "compass" towards a new type of democracy in China is to establish (1) a first-rate mechanism for selecting the right talents at all levels of the Chinese state; (2) a first-rate mechanism for exercising democratic supervision; and (3) a first-rate mechanism for carrying out extensive and intensive social consultations. With this broad orientation, China could encourage each region to carry out bold explorations and experiments and eventually shape a new democracy that is in line with China's own history and conditions and performs better than the Western democracy in really serving the interests of the people.

Second, reform should be demand-driven. The reform should proceed by meeting China's real domestic demand, rather than demands from other countries, and only the reform driven by effective domestic demand can be really useful and effective to the Chinese people. Effective domestic demand means the genuine demands originating from China's reality. Presently, China's greatest domestic demands are perhaps the development of an effective anti-corruption regime, an intra-Party democratic system, and a service-oriented government.

The third is the primacy of people's livelihood. To my mind, China's political reform should still serve the purpose of improving people's livelihood in a more meaningful and comprehensive way, including providing more and better services to the people and ensuring a higher quality of life and greater dignity for them. A key reason for the failures of Western-style democratization in developing countries is democratization for the sake of democratization, and political reform for the sake of political reform, often on terms dictated by the West. This has, not infrequently, resulted in endless domestic political wrangling, ethnic and religious clashes and even wars, rather than better lives for the people. As a country with a population four times larger than the US and more than the total population of the West, China's experiments and success in its political reform may eventually mark a paradigm shift and redefine what constitutes democracy and good governance. China's experimentation in this regard is bound to have lasting global implications.

5.2 Debating Human Rights

On February 9, 2010, I was invited by the Organizing Committee of the Geneva International Human Rights Film Festival to join a debate on human rights in China, and I accepted the invitation with pleasure. I knew that the Festival was rather critical of China's human rights record, but I had a lot to say on this issue. It was a full house with about 300 participants from all walks of life, mainly Geneva-based NGOs, diplomats and university lecturers and students, and the debate was heated, yet on the whole polite. I was surrounded by people with more questions after the debate, and I could not say that I convinced most people, but they perhaps got a better knowledge of how an educated Chinese looked at the whole range of human rights issues concerning China and beyond. The following is a summary of my response to various questions from the audience:

> Some of you have mentioned the supposed challenge posed by the rise of China to the international human rights regime, but my humble opinion runs just in the opposite direction: without the enormous progress in human rights and fundamental freedoms, it would be inconceivable for China to rise at such a scale and speed. A country with massive violation of human rights cannot be expected to rise so speedily. You may

pose a simple question to any Chinese you meet wherever you are, in Europe, China or the US: Are China's human rights better or worse today than in the past? I think most Chinese will answer that it's better now than anytime before.

China is the fastest-changing country in the world. What took Europe 300 years was condensed into 30–40 years, and this process inevitably has produced social tensions, including human rights issues, which call for an earnest solution, but most Chinese are satisfied with the direction in which their country is moving: according to a Pew survey conducted in 2008, 86% of the Chinese are satisfied as opposed to 23% in the US. So I think on matters relating to China, including human rights in China, it's necessary to first ask the Chinese, not Americans or Europeans.

It's mind-boggling for me that many in the West always believe that they know China better than the Chinese, Africa better than the Africans, Russia better than the Russians. This is wrong. Take Africa as an example. The West always thinks that democratization should be Africa's top priority, but it should at least ask the Africans themselves what they think about it. I have traveled to many African countries, and I can say that most Africans want first of all to solve such human rights issues as food, jobs, disease treatment and street safety, but the West asks them to place democratization above everything else, and in the end, how many of these countries end up in chaos?

No country in the world can realize all human rights simultaneously and there should be priorities in achieving human rights. China does not follow the Western preference and regards poverty eradication as a top-priority human right and hence has lifted over 400 million people out of poverty. Poverty eradication is not considered part of human rights in much of the West or the US, which even does not consider economic, social and cultural rights human rights, but we have no time to wait for the West to wake up. We have done it the Chinese way and achieved very positive results.

Just now, a question was raised about why China did not join the West in exercising sanctions against the alleged dictatorships in Africa. Here there is a conceptual difference. From the Chinese point of view, helping Africa get rid of poverty is a core human right, and no country should be allowed to violate this human right under whatever excuses. China's approach is similar to that of the Red Cross humanitarian assistance, with no regard to the classification of enemies or friends. If sanctions have to be applied, it must be done through the United Nations, rather than by a few Western countries. There are many human rights problems in the West. For instance, most of the Western countries have not yet practiced equal pay for equal work. Should other countries apply sanctions against these Western countries?

Democracy is a universal value, but the Western democratic system is not. The two things cannot be mixed up. The core value of democracy is to reflect the will of the people and achieve good governance. Whether it's one party, several parties or no party, a system is good if it delivers good governance, and it is not good if it fails to provide good governance. Looking around the world, I cannot find a single case where a non-Western country can adopt the Western political system and become a developed country.

The West itself should also reflect on its own political system. What's the main cause of the US financial crisis? What has happened to Europe's PIGS (Portugal, Italy, Greece and Spain)? What is the relationship between the financial crisis and Western democracy? To what extent has such a crisis undermined the human rights of the peoples of these countries and other countries? Why is the separation of power in the US political system unable to effectively prevent or tackle this crisis? I think that separation of power within the political domain alone can hardly be effective in this regard, and a modern state requires a broader balance beyond the political domain between political, capital and social forces. The fact that China was able to avoid the financial crash is inseparable from this kind of balance in China. If American democracy is still powerless in checking the overwhelming power of capital, the US may well encounter new crises in the years to come.

As for capital punishment, most Chinese, to my mind, do not support its abolition. This kind of public wish has to be respected, and this is the pre-condition of democracy. I sometimes ponder a related question, i.e. if the West genuinely cherishes life, including the lives of murderers, why doesn't the West go one step further and simply declare that peace is a universal value, and that no country has the right to launch wars against others unless authorized by the United Nations? How many innocent civilians have been killed in the Iraq War launched by the United States? At least 100,000. Doesn't it mean that over 100,000 innocent civilians have been sentenced to capital punishment? Is this not a gross violation of human rights?

Human rights are important, but many traditional values are equally important. The smooth functioning of a society requires an organic amalgamation of many elements. Like all other countries, there're corrupt officials, troublemakers and thugs in China, but most Chinese are sincere and kind people, and this character has been shaped by thousands of years of Chinese traditional values. Not long ago, huge natural disasters hit Haiti and New Orleans in the US, which were immediately followed by massive looting and other crimes. In contrast, this situation did not occur during China's Sichuan earthquake of 2008 which affected a population ten times larger. Why is this so? I think this has to do with Chinese traditional values, which are humanistic in nature, where a human being has to know how to help others in need and plundering a burning house is cursed by the heaven.

A few years ago, a pop song titled "Coming Home More Often" became an instant hit across China, as the song was deeply rooted in the Chinese idea of filial piety. Yet it also became controversial, because of the lyrics of the song: "Come home more often, to chat with your mom about issues of life, to chat with your dad about issues of work." Some feminist scholars argue that this song discriminates against women, but most Chinese do not share this view. They believe that China's pace of modernization is so fast that people have become extremely busy, but however busy, one should come home more often to see one's parents. This is heart-warming and has struck a chord with most Chinese. All societies have their respective cultural traditions, which, in China, took shape thousands of years ahead of the Western-defined human rights norms, and it's simply wrong to apply indiscriminately the Western-defined human rights concepts to different cultures and societies. International human rights norms should draw on different cultures and traditions so as to enrich themselves. In a nutshell, we should guard more against cultural absolutism in the world, rather than cultural relativism as mentioned by some of you earlier. We should guard against the inclination to consider one culture to possess universal values while treating other cultures as backward, and refrain from imposing one's culture on others.

When I was learning English as a student, my English teacher told me that in English, the word "I" was written with a capital letter, indicating the importance of "I" in life. The Chinese language does not distinguish between capital letters and small letters, and if there were such a distinction in Chinese, then not only I, but also you, we, he and she should all be written in capital letters. In Chinese culture, you are born into a social role as a son, a daughter, a father, a mother, a colleague of others, and rights and obligations are always linked. I genuinely feel that China's humanistic culture can enrich the Western individual-based concept of human rights. I also hold that the Chinese ancient civilization is in fact very postmodern and highly relevant for resolving many issues in the Western society and in tackling some major issues of global governance.

As for the question concerning Chinese dissidents, frankly speaking, they expect a color revolution in China, but what kind of result has the color revolutions brought to Ukraine, Georgia and Kyrgyzstan? It's none other than a disaster from my point of view. These people take Charter 77 and the Solidarity movement of Poland as their models, yet when all their demands have been realized in such a country like Haiti, the result is a completely failed state. The world has entered the 21st century and witnessed the disintegration of the former Soviet Union and ex-Yugoslavia and one failure after another of the color revolutions, but these people still talk in abstract terms about democracy and copying the Western political model. How can this be convincing? They should ask themselves why their cause enjoys so little support even among the overseas Chinese who have lived in the West for generations.

When I visited Poland four years ago, I checked a survey conducted by Pew, according to which 72% of Chinese were satisfied with their country, while 13% of Poles were satisfied with their country. If this is the case, who should learn from whom? I hope you will visit Gdansk, the birthplace of the Solidarity movement, and Warsaw, and then Shanghai, the birthplace of the Chinese workers' movement. You will see which place represents the future of the world. China was ahead of the West for at least over 1,000 years, but later China became complacent, and hence started lagging behind the West. But China has been striving hard to learn from others, including some practices of promoting human rights in the West, since 1978, yet China has not abandoned its own strong points. This is why China is making rapid progress, China's one year now perhaps equals ten years in the West, and the Chinese also look beyond the Western model. If the West is still complacent and only knows how to lecture others, it will feel regret one day.

With regard to the Western discourse on human rights as a whole, I also detect its weaknesses. First, it has difficulty keeping a balance between civil and political rights and economic, social and cultural rights. For instance, the American concept of human rights does not include economic, social and cultural rights. If the US could tackle the issue of nearly 50 million Americans without medical insurance from a human rights perspective, it would be perhaps much easier for the US to solve the issue. A 2011 Gallup survey shows that in fact almost one in five Americans (19%) say they did not have enough money for food in the past year as opposed to China's 6% (Fig. 5.1). I don't know when the American leadership and public will eventually wake up to this gap and start reforming America's human rights regime and perceptions.

Second, there is the problem of excessive legalism. In the West, human rights issues are essentially regarded as legal issues and usually only judiciable cases are viewed as human rights issues. This legalistic approach is difficult to apply in countries where legal traditions and institutions are weak and porous, and it is also extremely costly, especially for developing countries. A case in point is the Indian government's policy for compensation in slum clearance, which only compensates the slum owners for dismantling their slums. On the surface, it is based on the rule of law, yet most Indian slum dwellers are poor renters, rather than owners. As a result, it is very difficult to reduce slums or the homeless population in India. To my mind, it makes better sense that, at least in non-Western countries, while promoting the rule of law, one should also adopt political means to promote human rights, and this is an important experience in China's efforts to realize human rights.

Have there been times in the past 12 months when you did not have enough money to buy food that you or your family needed?

Percentage saying "yes"

■ China   ▓ United States

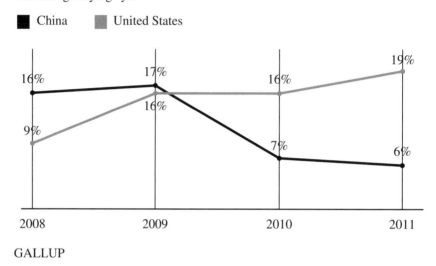

GALLUP

Figure 5.1 Gallup survey on the percentage of Chinese and Americans who felt they lacked enough money to buy food.

Excessive legalism also entails huge litigation costs, which, from my point of view, could turn out to be corruption in disguise or a kind of legalized corruption. For one thing, the rich can always hire more competent lawyers to win their cases than the poor, resulting in greater legal injustice. Excessive legalism tends to place undue emphasis on procedural correctness, which also leads to long delays and years of backlogs.

Third, there is the dilemma of individual rights vs. collective rights. The Western emphasis on individual rights has its rationale, i.e. its fear that collective rights may be achieved at the expense of individual rights, but this concern is faced with the same challenge, i.e. individual rights could also be pursued at the expense of collective rights, as in the case of the freedom of expression exercised by one individual Danish cartoonist that has affected the collective right of a billion Muslims to religious freedom. An ideal regime of human rights protection should strike a balance between individual and collective rights, between rights and responsibilities. In this regard, the Chinese holistic philosophical tradition is, I think, more compatible with the future trend of human rights norms in the world.

Fourth, it lacks a sense of sequence and priorities in exercising human rights. In fact, no country can achieve all human rights simultaneously. The West tends to give top priority to promoting political rights, but often with disastrous results in developing countries. In many poverty-stricken countries, giving priority to democratization leads to a situation of failed states like Haiti, where poverty causes chaos and anarchy, and eventually the country can only rely on the UN peacekeeping forces to restore peace and stability. Having the wrong sequence often produces the wrong results, and Western-style democratization often means voting along religious and ethnic lines in non-Western countries, leading, not infrequently, to chaos and even civil wars.

Human rights debates should not be treated as something for scoring political points; rather they are about how to apply the collective wisdom of mankind to tackle the multiplying global challenges. China is on the whole right to grasp the key issues and make economic development and poverty eradication the top priorities in promoting human rights, which in turn bring about social changes and lay a solid foundation for realizing other human rights. For a developing country, its limited resources have determined that it must have its own priorities in promoting human rights. For countries like Afghanistan and the Democratic Republic of the Congo, restoration of public order and economic development should be the top priorities for their human rights promotion, and if the international community can help the two countries achieve these targets within the next three to five years, it will already be a huge achievement in promoting human rights in the two countries.

It is true that certain human rights belong to core rights and universal values which are the shared bottom lines of all human civilizations, such as prohibition of torture and slavery, the right to independent thinking, and freedom from arbitrary arrest. There is no difference between the Chinese and the mainstream Western views on these rights. This is why the international community is stunned by the acts of torture committed by the US in the Guantanamo Bay prison, as these acts have violated the bottom line of a civilized society. Furthermore, universal values must be universally discussed, defined and endorsed by the international community, rather than simply by a minority of countries.

It would be ideal if all countries in the world could exchange their experiences in promoting and protecting human rights and make up for each other's deficiencies in this field. The world is multi-faceted and diverse, and even among the Western countries, human rights perceptions differ from country to country. For instance, high income tax is normal in Sweden, but may be considered in the United States an infringement of one's individual rights. Britain still retains a state religion, which is something inconceivable in a country like France that experienced the French Revolution, but the French government maintained its monopoly over television stations until 1982, something inconceivable in the United States. Likewise, the banning of Muslim headscarves in schools in France and other European countries is inconceivable in China.

Today's globalization has posed many challenges to the international community, which can only be tackled through genuine cooperation among nations in the world. According to American scholar Jared Diamond, at this stage the developed countries consume 32 times more resources than the developing ones, and the Americans consume 11 times more resources than the Chinese.[1] Yet the Western concept of human rights determines the belief that what the West has already enjoyed, including its lifestyle, is part of its inalienable human rights, and if other countries and peoples want to enjoy same rights and their corresponding share of resources, they will be subject to criticism and containment.

The Western political system is only accountable to the voters of individual countries, not to the peoples of other countries. How can such a self-centered system be accountable to the international community and help resolve the many pressing global issues such as climate change, trade protectionism and global poverty? China has a rich reservoir of humanistic culture and a belief that rights should be combined with responsibilities, and this, I think, can go a long way to enrich the Western concept of human rights. China will continue to draw on the good experiences of other countries and explore new frontiers in protecting and promoting

---

[1] Jared Diamond, "What's Your Consumption Factor?", *The New York Times*, January 2, 2008.

human rights and make its unique contributions to the global cause of human rights.

5.3 The Rise of a New Political Discourse

Critics of China, including the well-meaning ones, often claim that despite China's economic success since 1978, China has no big ideas to offer. But transforming a country the size of China has to follow certain ideas, some of which may have implications far beyond China's borders. Here are eight Chinese ideas:

(1) *Shishi qiushi* (Seeking Truth from Facts)

This is an ancient Chinese concept first raised in the *Hanshu* (History of Han Dynasty) written by famous historian Ban Gu (AD 32–92). It refers to having an honest attitude towards learning. By the Ming and Qing dynasties (from the 14th century onwards), it was reinterpreted as discovering rules through examining facts, and in English it is translated into "seeking truth from facts". Later Mao Zedong reinterpreted this idea as the axiom for the success of the Chinese revolution. When Deng Xiaoping came back to power in the late 1970s, he reiterated the need to "emancipate the mind and seek truth from facts" and re-established this idea as the guiding philosophy for China's reform and opening up.

Deng believed that facts rather than ideological dogmas, whether from the East or West, should serve as the ultimate criteria for assessing the correctness of a policy. This idea is in line with the concept of reason during the Enlightenment of Europe, as both ideas broke away from the rigid ideological straitjacket of the past and emphasized human capacity for reasoning and ushered in the respective industrial revolutions.

But there are also differences between the two ideas. As "seeking truth from facts" in today's context is a product of the interactions between China's ancient civilization and modern civilizations, it has avoided such historical limitations as racism or Euro-centrism associated with the concept of reason of that era. It requires all human activities to be assessed through social practices, and the criterion for such assessment is to what extent they keep with the overall interests of the people.

Thanks to this idea, China's rise has been a peaceful one, without bringing wars to the world like the rise of the European powers did in the past. Rather, it has brought about opportunities for development to the Chinese and other peoples. With this idea, China has also become arguably the least "ideological" power in the world and is ready to draw on whatever is good in other countries, thus paving the way for China's progress on virtually all fronts.

Through examining facts, Beijing found that neither the Soviet communist model nor the Western liberal democratic model has really worked for a developing country in terms of achieving genuine modernization, and it was thus determined to explore its own path of development. It eventually succeeded in finding its own path, which is by no means perfect, but has allowed China to achieve far greater successes than most other countries over the past three decades.

This idea has enabled China to adopt a pragmatic, experimental and "trial-and-error" approach to its reform, and in the process shaped its own largely successful model of development. The idea reminds China and the rest of the world of the need to reject ideological dogmas, such as the dogma about liberal democracy being the end of history. No, history is not ending, just unfolding in a big way, and all countries should be encouraged to look at the real conditions of their own countries and explore their own paths of development.

(2) *Minsheng weida* (Primacy of People's Livelihood)

As stated before, the Chinese long hold the view that people's livelihood constitutes the cornerstone of a country. A key message from China's reform and opening up is that a developing country or the government of such a country should devote itself to eradicating poverty and improving people's living standards.

This idea has underpinned China's success in lifting over 400 million individuals out of abject poverty in less than three decades, an unprecedented success in human history. China may be arguably correcting a historical neglect in the range of human rights advocated by the West which has focused almost exclusively on civil and political rights since the Enlightenment. One reason for this neglect is perhaps that leading

European thinkers of that era represented Europe's rising middle class at a time when the worst form of poverty, including slavery, was occurring in the European colonies, rather than Europe itself. Widespread poverty in the world today makes a mockery of basic human dignity and all civil liberties, and should be treated as an unacceptable violation of the most basic individual rights.

While the West accuses China of not caring about human rights in its relations with Africa, China believes that poverty is the root cause of many evils, including terrorism, and fighting poverty itself should be treated as a non-derogatory core human right, and no country should use any excuse, including that of promoting democracy or eradicating corruption, to derail efforts aimed at fighting poverty.

The Western political model in non-Western countries often fails to eradicate poverty. Frankly speaking, the Chinese model is by no means perfect, as it has its own weaknesses, but the Western model has performed too poorly in the developing world, where most people find little chance to get out of poverty. It is therefore likely that the Chinese model will become more appealing to the world's poor.

(3) *Zhengti siwei* (Holistic Thinking)

Influenced by China's holistic philosophical tradition, Beijing tends to reject a piecemeal approach to China's development and is inclined towards long-term strategic planning. Holistic thinking is important as the whole is viewed as larger than the combination of its parts. It is in this context that China has mapped out a 70-year long-term strategy for modernization since the early 1980s, and has unswervingly pursued it till this day.

The holistic thinking is also revealed in how China has tried to achieve such values as individual rights, happiness, freedom and dignity. These are all considered individual values in the West, yet in the Chinese political culture, these values are both individual and collective, linked with the peace and stability of the nation, in part because China experienced too many chaos and wars in its long history, and people tend to view "peace under the heaven" as the top mandate of any competent central government. The family-oriented tradition has also evolved a tradition of linking the individual family with the fate of the country, which is viewed as a large overarching family for all. Most Chinese therefore tend to view seriously the prosperity and dignity of their country as something inseparable from individual safety, happiness, freedom and dignity.

The Chinese experience shows that a tradition, whether from the East or West, may always have its strengths and weaknesses. What we should do is to highlight its strengths while minimizing its weaknesses. When the Chinese holistic approach is used correctly, it is far more effective than the Western individual approach in realizing many individual values.

If China only follows in the footsteps of the West, where individualism is the norm, China may forever be left behind by the West. But once China gives play to its strengths by promoting individual values and interests through a holistic approach, China tends to achieve better results than with the Western approach, as demonstrated in China's approach to hosting the Olympic Games. The Games were organized with a state-led holistic approach and brought spectacular results both for the state and for countless individuals who were mobilized to take up sports to keep fit. The same was with the World Expo of 2010 held in Shanghai, where a state-led holistic approach was also taken, which has inspired countless individuals to appreciate what constitutes low-carbon urban life.

This approach can be called Deng Xiaoping's approach, which contrasts sharply with what can be called Mother Teresa's individualistic approach in India. While Deng's has lifted over 400 million individuals out of poverty who have in turn achieved more individual rights, Mother Teresa's has touched many and won her the Nobel Peace Prize, but India's overall poverty remains largely unchanged. For developing countries, holistic thinking is perhaps more important, as they have far less resources than the developed countries, and without a sense of priorities, their chance of achieving modernization is very slim.

Holistic thinking has enabled China to establish a clear pattern of priorities at different stages of China's transformation, and this long-term holistic approach contrasts sharply with short-termism and narrow and populist politics so prevalent today in both the West and other parts of the world. Mankind is faced with multiplying challenges which are global in nature and call for global and holistic solutions. But the dilemma now is that given the nature of the Western political system, politicians are essentially held responsible only to their own constituencies at home, not to other peoples and nations. For instance, few politicians in the West would be able to advocate a carbon tax on gasoline consumption in the interest of fighting global warming and get votes. Former US President Jimmy Carter suffered immediately at the polls after asking Americans to cut their energy consumption.[2] Indeed, I think that China's holistic thinking points in the right direction for resolving many issues of global governance.

(4) *Zhengfu shi biyaodeshan* (Government as a Necessary Virtue)

Contrary to the orthodox American view of the state as a necessary evil, prosperous times in China's long history were usually associated with a strong and enlightened state. China's vast territory and large and diverse population shaped a tradition of a strong central government for tackling frequently occurring natural disasters and coordinating diverse regional interests. A strong state is part and parcel of Chinese history, buttressed by its long tradition and practice of a merit-based mandarin system. The tradition of a strong state has both advantages, such as concentrated power for implementing large projects, and disadvantages, such as a tendency towards state monopolies.

China's transformation has been led by a strong and pro-development state. Contrary to Mikhail Gorbachev, who abandoned the old state which then led to his country's disintegration, Deng Xiaoping reoriented the Chinese state from pursuing utopia to promoting China's modernization, with significant success. The Chinese state is, imperfect as it is, capable of shaping a national consensus on modernization, ensuring overall stability for development, and pursuing long-term strategic objectives. In contrast, the Russians paid a heavy price for Gorbachev's effort to start a new state from scratch, and without Vladimir Putin's efforts, however controversial they are, Russia's further disintegration may well have been inevitable.

The Chinese approach has its own weaknesses but its strengths far outweigh them, and China's rapid rise is inseparable from a strong state. In fact, even the US, a country long suspicious of the role of the state, has

---

[2] Michael Tomasky, "The Untransformational President", *Newsweek*, August 15, 2011, p. 15.

resorted to large-scale state intervention during the financial crisis, and this is dubbed by some as "socialism with American characteristics".

In the world today, where the rules of the game are mostly shaped by the West, it is difficult to imagine how, without a strong state, a developing country can develop and prosper. Some Chinese scholars talk at length about the market economy with perfect competition, but they apparently fail to understand that the world markets from food to oil experience innumerable speculative attacks all the time originating from the West. Where are we to find a perfect market in the world other than in economics textbooks? The whole economy of a country may well be swallowed up by such merciless and destructive speculators, and China's strong state provides a layer of protection for the Chinese economy and society.

Not long ago, EU Commissioner Stavros Dimas talked about how to practice adaptations with regard to climate change and concluded that fighting climate change is like fighting battles, and the state should be encouraged to play a bigger role. In retrospect, the whole process of China's reform and opening up has been a series of state-guided battles from agricultural reform to the special economic zones to the coastal development strategies to the accession to the WTO to the hosting of the Olympic Games and the World Expo to the ongoing restructuring of the economy. Victories in these battles have laid the foundation for China's spectacular rise today, and the Chinese concept and practice of state intervention are now being closely studied by many other countries at this time of global economic crisis.

Naturally, from the viewpoint of state governance, the Chinese state is also faced with the task of reforming itself, especially in such fields as self-regulation, anti-corruption, readjustment of relations between enterprises, state and society and the effective supervision of the state. China still needs to explore new ways and means in this regard in the years to come, but the importance of "state as a necessary virtue" in modernization is crucial for China and perhaps for many other countries as well.

(5) *Liangzheng shanzhi* (Good Governance)

The Chinese idea of *liangzheng shanzhi* or good governance in English is another key concept. While there is still no internationally accepted consensus on what constitutes "good governance", the Chinese idioms of *yirenweiben* and *lijingtuzhi*, or "striving hard for human-centered good governance" seem to explain how most Chinese understand the concept.

The relative success of China since 1978 shows that whatever the political system, it must in the end boil down to good governance. In other words, the ultimate test of a good political system is to what extent it can ensure good governance. The stereotyped dichotomy of democracy vs. autocracy sounds increasingly hollow in today's complex world, given the large numbers of poorly governed "democracies". China's idea may eventually shape a paradigm shift from the dichotomy of democracy vs. autocracy to that of good governance vs. bad governance.

Good governance may take the form of the Western political system as in the case of perhaps Switzerland, or the form of a non-Western political system as in the case of Singapore and Hong Kong. China, with all its shortcomings, is a much better-governed country than most developing countries. Likewise, bad governance may take the form of the Western political system as in the case of Haiti, Iraq, Mongolia, Ukraine and the recently bankrupt Iceland and Greece, and it may also take the form of a non-Western political system as in the case of Burma.

It follows that, from the Chinese point of view, the nature of a state, including its legitimacy, has to be defined more by its substance, i.e. good governance, than by its procedures. China emphasizes substance over procedures, believing that ultimately the right substance will evolve into the right procedures, appropriate to each nation's own conditions, just as the West believes in the reverse. Good governance should be an objective of all governments in the world, and the developing world is faced with the mounting challenge of political reform in order to achieve good governance. The same is true for the developed world.

(6) *Minxin xiangbei and xuanxian renneng* (Winning the Hearts and Minds of the People and Meritocracy)

As a civilizational state, the Chinese idea on regime legitimacy is also unique and can be traced back to ancient times. The legitimacy of the Chinese regime comes from two ancient concepts. One is *minxin* or *minxin xiangbei*, and its approximate English translation is "winning or losing the hearts and minds of the people". The concept was first put forward by Mencius (372–289 BC), and *minxin* is different from the concept of *minyi* (public opinion), as public opinion can be fleeting and change overnight. *Minxin* refers more to the whole and long-term interest of a nation and is therefore more stable and lasting.

Under this concept, China has a long tradition of moral premonition to the rulers that unless they work diligently, they may risk losing the "hearts and minds of the people" and hence their "mandate of heaven". This premonition is part of the core doctrine of Mencius with its impact on Chinese officialdom continuing to this day.

Perhaps the very size of the country and population has shaped this Chinese perception of regime legitimacy, and it is simply unimaginable that most Chinese will ever accept a change of central government every four or five years as practiced in the so-called modern multi-party democracy in the West. An inaccurate yet revealing analogy could be that if the Roman Empire had continued to survive till this day, one wonders if it could have withstood the test of this kind of multi-party system and popular democracy without risking its own breakup and demise.

The other concept is *xuanxian renneng,* and its literal English translation is "selecting the virtuous and appointing the able" or simply "meritocracy". The concept originated from *xuanxian juneng* (selecting the virtuous and recommending the able) as contained in *Li Ji* or *Book of Rites* complied in the early Han Dynasty (202–9 BC). The Chinese invention of the *Keju* system or national civil servant exam embodies this idea of selecting leaders through exams and performances. As Henry Kissinger has observed, "China had for well over one thousand years a fully formed imperial bureaucracy recruited by competitive examination, permeating and regulating all aspects of the economy and society."[3] The *Keju* system generally ensured the selection of relatively competent leaders to work for the Chinese government at all levels and produced a quality of governance unmatched in Europe for at least 1,000 years.

Political scientist Pan Wei has made a good point that in China's long history, an enlightened emperor represented a dynasty with a mandate of heaven, and his dynasty was run by a united Confucian ruling elite selected

---

[3] Henry Kissinger, *On China,* Penguin, New York, 2011, p. 16.

on the basis of meritocracy. The mandate of a good dynasty lasted for several hundreds of years, longer than the whole US history. The Communist Party of China (CPC) in many ways still continues this tradition of the mandate of heaven, which in today's context is to revitalize the Chinese nation. The CPC is not the Republican or Democratic Party of the US, which openly represent certain group interests of the society. The CPC, in its Confucian ruling tradition, represents the interests of the whole nation, and most Chinese perceive it the same way. Pan Wei argues further that in the Chinese political culture, people usually perceive negatively any party politics.[4]

In China's long history, dynastic change was often violent, causing heavy losses of life and property to the people. As a result, most Chinese detest frequent changes of dynasties and favor constant reforms within a dynasty rather than constant revolutions. This kind of political tradition provides a unique perspective for us to understand the nature of the Chinese political system today and the cycles of China's political change. It has also placed China, from my point of view, in a better position to compete with the Western model and overcome such defects as short-termism and populist politics so prevalent in the West.

Inspired by the Confucian tradition of meritocracy, Beijing practices, though not always successfully, performance legitimacy across the whole political strata. Criteria such as performance in poverty eradication and, increasingly, a cleaner environment are key factors in the promotion of officials. China's top leaders are generally competent and well tested at different levels of responsibility.

Performance legitimacy raises a concern that if one's performance is not as good as expected or the economy goes sour, legitimacy may be lost. Yet the reality is that most Chinese are fair-minded: if you have had good performance in the past, and if you are still working earnestly for the people, they tend to understand you and give you room for improvement. In fact, crises often provide opportunities for consolidating legitimacy. Mere procedural legitimacy is almost comparable to a student registering himself for his class but never bothering to perform. In the case of China,

---

[4] Pan Wei and Ma Ya (eds.), 《人民共和国60年与中国模式》 (60 Years of the People's Republic and the China Model), SDX Joint Publishing Company, Beijing, 2010, pp. 11–16.

such a student has not only to register himself but also to perform well in the exams; otherwise he will have to quit his class.

Hong Kong-based political commentator Frank Ching once cited my argument about the Chinese view of political governance, and observed, "Without denying the remarkable progress China has made in recent decades and the support of the Chinese people, there is a logical problem with those who argue in favour of an authoritarian government. What if, one day, the Chinese government should lose the support of the majority of China's people [...]? Will it step down [...]?"[5]

This is a pertinent question, and here I would like to quote the rebuttal from Eric Li, a political commentator based in Shanghai. Li noted that Frank Ching was "comparing an apple to an orange" and China's political system is "enshrined in its constitution [*author's note*: and rooted in its long history], just as liberal democracy is in the US constitution". He further observed that Ching's assertion would mean that "in a hypothetical situation in which the system of liberal electoral democracy no longer has popular support in America, the US must do away with elections, cancel the Bill of Rights [...]. If unfortunate developments lead to the loss of popular support for either constitutional system, it would take nothing short of a revolution to overthrow them, or sustained periods of national malaise without one".[6]

From a long-term perspective, a system based solely on public opinions (minyi) and simple-minded populism may lose out in competition to a system based on both public opinions (minyi) and the "hearts and minds of the people". This is why the Chinese idea of *minxin xiangbei*, meritocracy and performance legitimacy will, from my point of view, generate lasting international implications.

(7) *Jianshou bingxu* (Selective Learning and Adaptation)

China represents a secular culture where learning from others is prized. The Chinese have developed a remarkable capacity for selective learning and adaptation to new challenges, and China's official slogan is to build a

---

[5] Frank Ching, "The China Model's Inherent Flaw", *The Globe and Mail*, August 25, 2011.
[6] Eric Li, "Letters to the Editor", *The Globe and Mail*, August 30, 2011.

learning-minded state and society. As a result, a system of learning has been set up at all levels of the party and state from grassroots workplaces to the top leadership of the Political Bureau. China has thus drawn on the experience of other countries in virtually all areas of modernization, ranging from enterprise management to state functioning to highway construction and the promotion of science and technology.

It is important to note that in this process of learning from others, China has managed to maintain its own independent policy space. For instance, China has learnt a lot from the West in the financial and monetary sector, yet it has maintained state control over major banks and adopted a rather prudent stand on liberalizing China's capital market. As a result, China has successfully conducted its banking sector reforms yet avoided the global financial crash. China has embraced the IT revolution and even excelled in it, and China has gained immensely from joining the WTO through a large-scale controlled learning and adaptation process.

In comparison, the West seems to be rather complacent. Some in the West still believe that their system represents the end of history, but complacence leads to decline. Take the US as an example. It declined for eight years running under the George W. Bush administration and is now experiencing the most serious recession since the 1930s. Europe is also mired in economic malaise and political rigidity. Much of the developing world is also faced with crises, and many of them have followed blindly the Western model only to find themselves in one crisis after another. In this world of fierce international competition, a nation can only stand firm and grow when it is able to keep its policy space while constantly learning from others and adapting itself to changing circumstances.

(8) *Hexie zhongdao* (Harmony and Moderation)

This is in many ways a hallmark of Chinese culture. The Chinese generally value harmony over confrontation and moderation over extremism, and the Confucian idea of "harmony in diversity" is often the goal of an ideal society, where there are "three harmonies ", i.e. a person's internal harmony, harmony among humans and harmony between humans and nature. Behind these harmonies is the very Chinese concept of unity of opposites, i.e, *yin* and *yang*, or unity of female-related forces and male-related forces, as elaborated in the *I Ching* (Book of Changes) written over 2,000 years ago. The ideas of *zhongdao* and *zhongyong,* or the art of achieving balance and harmony in life and with nature, first elaborated on in a book *Zhong Yong* (The Doctrine of the Mean) around 200 BC.

Harmony and moderation do not necessarily mean complacency and passivity; rather they refer more to "seeking common ground while reserving differences" and to achieving what Confucius called *he'erbutong* or "harmony in diversity". This tradition has allowed different religions in China to co-exist and even mingle with each other in China's long history, and spared China from the innumerable religious wars prevalent in European history. The success of China's reform and opening up since 1978 is also inseparable from Beijing's firm belief in moderation and gradual reform, rather than in extremism and shock therapy.

As China rises, social tensions also multiply, but China rejects the Western concept of adversarial politics in the belief that seeking common ground while reserving differences is crucial in handling different social interests. Given the fact that the Western model of adversarial politics in non-Western countries is in deep trouble and in the West itself in disarray, even a liberal intellectual like Francis Fukuyama writes that "US democracy has little to teach China"[7] and it is only natural that China will continue to proceed in its own way.

Beyond China, the ideas of harmony and moderation may also represent some hope for tackling many intractable global challenges. Many in the West thought that with the removal of the Berlin Wall in 1989, all world issues would be resolved through liberal democracy, and this proved to be short-sighted. The world has been witnessing more walls rising up since then: the wall between rich and poor, between haves and have-nots, between cultures and between civilizations.

Who should be held responsible for the rise of these walls? Singaporean academic Kishore Mahbubani notes, "There is a fundamental flaw in the West's strategic thinking. In all its analyses of global challenges, the West assumes that it is the source of the solutions to the world's key problems.

---

[7] Francis Fukuyama, "US Democracy Has Little to Teach China", *Financial Times,* January 17, 2011.

In fact, however, the West is also a major source of these problems. Unless key Western policymakers learn to understand and deal with this reality, the world is headed for an even more troubled phase."[8]

If there is any chance to resolve or at least mitigate the impact of some global challenges, one may have to draw on the Chinese ideas of harmony and moderation. Indeed, as global crises of all sorts further intensify, the international community may have no alternative but to show solidarity and help each other out of crises, and such solidarity can only be built on the basis of "harmony and moderation" and on respecting the political and cultural diversity of this troubled world.[9]

The eight ideas elaborated here, some may argue, are just appropriate for China or for China's current stage of development, and that as China further develops, China may also embrace liberal democracy. But it is more likely that China will further evolve along these ideas, which may or may not confront the Western values. As the world struggles to tackle the multiplying challenges, mankind needs new ideas beyond those of the West.

As far as China is concerned, it should examine in a critical way, in the light of China's own ideas, values and successful experiences, all the ideas, concepts and standards shaped or defined by the West such as democracy, human rights, freedom, the rule of law, the multi-party system, autocracy, the market economy, the role of the state, civil society, public intellectuals, GDP, the Gini coefficient and the human development index. China should draw on whatever is correct in them and reject whatever is erroneous and enrich or redefine them if need be, and in this process shape China's own discourse and standards.

The China model itself sets standards which are by no means perfect, but are already impacting the world at large: from the way China hosted the Olympic Games and the World Expo to how China builds highways and bullet trains; from eradicating poverty to fighting natural disasters; from initiating massive urban renewal to preventing economic and financial crises; from reforming the state-owned enterprises to developing

---

[8] Kishore Mahbubani, "The Case Against the West", *Foreign Affairs*, May/June (2008).

[9] For a brief summary of these ideas, see Zhang Weiwei, "Eight Ideas Behind China's Success", *The New York Times*, October 1, 2009.

alternative energies; from helping Africa to mapping out long-term strategies for its own national development. These standards are still evolving, but they have already stunned, in a way more positive than negative, many countries to the realization that many things in the world can be done in a different way from the Western approach.

Over the past century and more, China has learnt so much from the West, and will continue to do so for its own benefit. But it is perhaps also time for the West to learn about China's ideas and to see if the West can benefit from them. The Chinese ideas, especially those well tested as mentioned earlier, may indeed enrich mankind's collective wisdom in how to better tackle the multiplying global challenges.

CHAPTER 6

THE END OF THE END OF HISTORY

6.1 The Western Model: from India to Eastern Europe

When comparisons have to be made between China and other countries, one often thinks of India, as both countries achieved their independence in the late 1940s and both started at a similar level of development, with India slightly ahead of China, because China had endured almost continual wars and destruction for nearly a century, with a death toll running as high as several tens of millions.

But 60 years later, the gap between the two Asian giants could not be larger: China's economy is three times that of India; with less arable land, China's grain production is double that of India; China's foreign trade volume is four times larger; the average life span in China ten years longer; China's infant mortality three times lower; and India's economic and financial center Mumbai looks three decades behind its Chinese counterpart Shanghai.

Although many in the West wish India to outperform China, arguing that India's democratic system is its trump card, to this author, this trump card is of dubious and poor quality, and India's gap with China is likely to grow further, as behind the gap is a huge difference in the quality of the political system, and China is a much better-governed country than India.

Indeed, compared with China, India's democracy has to a great extent prevented India from conducting effective land reforms, indispensable to improving the lot of India's vast rural poor. For the same reason, India has failed to carry out women's liberation on the scale China has done, nor is

India able, not only in words, but also in deeds, to abolish the caste system, which affects about 160 million untouchables in the country. My fundamental question about India is that without a significant reform of its political system, how can India bring about these social changes, and without such social changes, how can India build a first-rate modern state based on good governance and overall prosperity?

I have observed five inherent weaknesses in India's democracy which constrain India's capacity for modernization. These weaknesses can be summarized as the double P's (politicization and populism) and the triple S's (soft state, short-termism and schisms).

First, Indian politics is to a great extent marked by the politicization of everything, and consequently it is hardly possible to discuss and tackle issues in an honest and matter-of-fact way. Even in matters such as investigating the causes of various terrorist attacks in Mumbai in recent years, different political parties have, or are widely perceived to have, their own agendas, and are therefore unable to reach a consensus necessary for effectively attacking the causes of terrorism.

Second, populism prevails. Indian politics is replete with examples of political parties competing with each other in promising individual benefits such as loan waivers, free power, social welfare and rice at 2 rupees, and politicians regard voters as commodities to be purchased in a political marketplace. This kind of competitive populism wins more voters, but sacrifices India's long-term and overall interests as it can hardly tackle India's many fundamental challenges such as the acute shortage of critical community and infrastructure assets.

Third, India's "soft state" (in the words of Nobel laureate Karl Gunnar Myrdal) does not allow the country to carry out much-needed institutional reforms or execute with reasonable efficiency many needed reform programs. The state is easily hijacked by various vested interest groups, as shown by the repeated failures in its attempts to handle the problem of slums or implement family planning policies, which, in most cases, hurt India's overall public interests.

Fourth, short-term politics thrive. Few politicians can look beyond his or her immediate term of office or election needs, and there is no way to conceive or pursue, as China does, a coherent nationwide reform program with a clear sense of the priorities and sequence.

Fifth, the four weaknesses stated above combined create schisms and disunity across the Indian society. It is a kind of laxity, or an absence of political will to shape a national consensus on nation-building. As India's democracy is premised on the idea of opposition for the sake of opposition, ethnic, religious and communal infighting thrives to the degree of creating extensive schisms and disunity across the society. Hence there is a clear lack of political will to get things done. If a major infrastructure project is required, it is inevitably delayed due to political wrangling of all sorts. This kind of schism seriously stunts India's progress.

Another category of countries that merit our special attention are the former socialist countries or transitional economies, particularly those in Eastern Europe. To apply a broad brush, my impression from visiting almost all the Eastern European countries over the past two decades is that China has outperformed them by a big margin, although their starting point was higher than China's.

Of these countries, Albania and Moldova are still poor developing countries, and political change has not brought about much-needed economic prosperity, and the two remain the least developed countries in Europe.

Other Eastern European countries are better off. The eight new members of the European Union (Estonia, Latvia, Lithuania, Poland, the Czech Republic, Slovakia, Bulgaria and Romania) all were mid-level industrialized countries prior to 1989, with a rural population smaller than 30% of the total population (compared to China's which is around 50% now), and East Germany, the Czech Republic and Hungary were much richer than Slovakia, Romania and Bulgaria.

I have visited all Eastern European countries except Estonia since 2000, but only their capitals, and it is therefore difficult to make a comprehensive comparison between these countries and China. In general, the capitals of these countries look prosperous with a sizable middle class, and aid and investments from the EU have played a role in the development of these countries. But if one compares these metropolises with China's first-tier cities like Shanghai, they are generally less developed. In particular, cities like Warsaw, Budapest, Bucharest, Sofia, Bratislava and Riga clearly lag behind Shanghai in terms of infrastructure, commercial prosperity, fashion as well as the scale, quality and design of the new urban architecture.

In Eastern Europe, the most attractive buildings are those left over from the era of the 19th and early 20th centuries, and their scale of urban renovation is much smaller than in any cities in China's developed regions. This may also mean that Eastern Europe had built enough residential housing for its citizens during the old era, while China had to build a lot of new residential areas to make up for the insufficient housing supply prior to 1978. China's scale of urban renewal and new metropolitan skylines are what few Eastern European countries can match.

On the whole, there was a big gap in terms of development between China and Eastern Europe three decades ago, but this gap has significantly narrowed. Twenty years ago cities like Warsaw and Budapest were a decade ahead of Shanghai, but now they seem a decade behind, if not more. On the whole, China's developed regions have caught up with or surpassed Eastern Europe, but it will take more time for the whole country to do the same.

Over the past 20 years, most Eastern European countries have followed what I call the two shock therapies during their transitions. Politically, they pursued shock therapy and shifted radically from communist rule to a Western-style multi-party democracy. Economically, they were guided by Western advisers and adopted shock therapy to ensure speedy privatization and liberalization. This approach is, however, widely viewed now in Eastern Europe and beyond as too costly, and most of these countries experienced hyperinflation up to 2000% and a sharp decline in living standards in the 1990s, a situation that was not reversed until the late 1990s. Now, the financial crisis has once again plunged much of Eastern Europe into crisis.

I do not mean that most people in Eastern Europe want to return to the old days. No, this is not the case, and few people in the world would like to turn their clocks back by 20 years, except perhaps war-torn Somalia, which I visited over 20 years ago. But if the people of Eastern Europe were allowed to have another chance for change, most of them would perhaps prefer a less radical and more gradual approach.

Many Eastern Europeans are saddened by the fact that their economies have become entirely dependent on the West. The process of radical privatization was immensely corrupt and people experienced enormous hardships. Today, their economies, including banking and some other key sectors, are nearly all controlled by Western companies, something inconceivable for China, and Eastern Europe has been particularly hard-hit by the 2008 global financial crash, given their high dependency on the Western economies.

Politically, Eastern European democracy has failed to deliver what most people want. The people's trust in the government and politicians is low, and the people's passion for radical change has largely evaporated and been replaced by widespread disillusionment with the existing political institutions. In contrast to the euphoria of 1989 is today's popular resentment and cynicism, and the following survey findings may illustrate the real situation today in Eastern Europe: the people's trust in the government is very low (Table 6.1); the quality of democracy is even lower than in Taiwan (Table 6.2); and their economic competitiveness is far behind China's (Table 6.3).

Table 6.1 People's trust in the government in Eastern Europe

Hungary	21%
Czech Republic	21%
Romania	21%
Latvia	19%
Poland	17%
Bulgaria	16%

Source: Eurobarometer, 2008.

Table 6.2 Ranking of the quality of Eastern European democracy as compared with Taiwan's

Czech Republic	18
Taiwan	32
Estonia	33
Hungary	38
Slovakia	41
Latvia	43
Poland	46
Bulgaria	49
Romania	50

Source: EIU, 2006.

Table 6.3 Economic competitiveness as compared with China's

China	15
Estonia	22
Lithuania	31
Slovakia	34
Hungary	35
Bulgaria	41
Romania	44
Poland	52

Source: *World Competitiveness Yearbook*, 2007, IMD.

Most Chinese from the Chinese mainland tend to think the quality of democracy in Taiwan is low, and according to this EIU survey, only the Czech Republic's quality of democracy is better than Taiwan's. But even in the Czech Republic, as my visit in 2008 revealed to me, most Czechs were rather disillusioned with the quality of Czech democracy. Jiří Dienstbier, the former foreign minister of the Czech Republic, observed in an op-ed piece in *The New York Times* in October 2006: "Citizens' dissatisfaction is growing everywhere, and participation rates in elections are dwindling, while public confidence in government, Parliament and the whole political process is ebbing away."[1]

Indeed, these findings largely tally with my field observations in these countries. Twenty years have passed since the 1989 revolution, yet these countries are still beset with building real democracies. Large numbers of petty politicians rival each other for personal gains, espousing nationalism, ethnic bigotry and economic populism, rather than working honestly for the interests of their peoples, despite all the money and assistance from the EU for building democracy. For many in Eastern Europe, there is only democracy in form, not in substance, and there are no real democrats, not to mention statesmen, and this is the main reason why most people are disillusioned with their "elected leaders". For most Eastern Europeans, their 1989 return to the European cultural space which they always

---

[1] Jiři Dienstbier, "Sweet and Sour Fruits of the Velvet Revolution", *The New York Times*, October 9, 2006.

belonged to was a dream coming true, but the path towards a new society seems more like a process from dream to disillusionment.

Eastern Europe is much closer to the West than China in cultural and political traditions and much smaller than China in terms of territory and population, but its two decades of performance in practicing Western-style democracy is still very much below the expected standards. Here the lesson for China is clear: as a country with entirely different cultural and political traditions from the West, any attempt to reproduce the Western political and economic model in China is likely to produce worse results than in Eastern Europe.

A good friend of mine, who is Hungarian and used to be passionate about popular democracy, told me in 2009 that he was fed up with the elections in Hungary, and he asserted that the best thing he could do now was to choose a less bad guy from two very bad guys. As Hungary was hit hard by the current financial tsunami, he lamented to me, "What can we do now? Hungary is waiting for rescue from the IMF, and the IMF is waiting for rescue from China." This is an exaggeration, but he may have pointed to an iota of truth. I remember in 1989 when the political storm hit Eastern Europe; the West was in euphoria, but Deng Xiaoping cautioned a visiting American guest, "Don't rejoice too soon, as the situation (in Eastern Europe) was complicated enough."[2] He urged China to adhere to its own path of development. Twenty years have passed by now, and China has had its share of problems, but few people doubt today that China's overall performance is much better than Eastern Europe's, and the Chinese have also learnt some useful lessons from the experience of Eastern Europe.

6.2 The Western Model: East Asia and Beyond

Two types of countries and societies have applied the Western political model in much of East Asia: the first are those embracing the Western model when they are still poor developing countries, such as the Philippines, Thailand and Mongolia, and the second are those adopting the Western political model after they have reached a higher level of modernization, such

---

[2] Deng Xiaoping, *Deng Xiaoping Wenxuan* (Selected Works of Deng Xiaoping), Vol. 3, People's Press, Beijing, p. 360.

as South Korea and Taiwan. But the quality of all these democracies leaves much to be desired, and they have all encountered at least three challenges often faced by non-Western societies copying the Western political model.

First, society becomes more divided. In Thailand, the past five years have witnessed continuous confrontations between the Red Shirts, that represent the more urban middle class, and the Yellow Shirts, that represent the poor, mostly in the countryside after the toppling of Prime Minister Thaksin Shinawatra. Behind this confrontation is Thailand's huge gap between the rich and poor, one of the largest in the world: the richest 20% owns more than 60% of the national income while the poorest 20% owns less than 5%.[3]

If the Thai situation can be described as an "urban-rural divide", where the urban middle class topples the populist leader elected by the rural poor, then Taiwan is a case of a "north-south divide", where supposedly pro-independence southerners are confronting the northerners who are perceived to have more sympathy with the idea of China. Pro-independence politicians in all their election campaigns create tensions between the so-called Taiwanese and the mainlanders as an effective way to win votes. Taiwan's leader Ma Ying-jeou is now trying to rebuild Taiwan's social cohesion but it is by no means easy given the degree of animosity between various social groups.

Kyrgyzstan is another case of a "north-south divide", and the so-called color revolution in 2005 was a victory for the southerners against the northerners, but President Aliyev failed to govern the country well and was overthrown in April 2010 by the forces in favor of the northerners. This confrontation caused large-scale bloody clashes and forced China to airlift its citizens back home.

Greater social divisions or "regional divides" have also occurred in South Korea after democratization. Korean politicians try to play up their "regional identities" as a way to win more votes, which has intensified existing differences between various provinces in the country.[4]

---

[3] Stanley A. Weiss, "Thailand's Lessons in Populism", *International Herald Tribune*, January 15, 2009.

[4] Lin Zhen, "台湾和韩国民主化比较研究" (A Comparative Study of Democratization in Taiwan and South Korea), www.tecn.cn/data.

Table 6.4   Corruption index

	Taiwan	Thailand	Mongolia	Philippines	Indonesia
2004	35	64	85	102	133
2008	39	80	102	141	126

Source: Transparency International website.

All these divisions have created political chaos of all sorts in these societies. Thailand's bloody clashes and chaos have continued on and off for four years and may flash up again. The Philippines has experienced many coup d'états over the past decades. Taiwan has experienced several assassination attempts and a million-strong Red Shirt protest against Chen Shui-bian. With a population of a little over 5 million, smaller than any of China's medium-sized cities, Kyrgyzstan is still politically divisive and unstable.

Second, corruption has generally increased, rather than decreased. It is often assumed that corruption declines with Western-style democracy, but judging from the corruption index compiled by Transparency International in 2004 and 2008, the opposite seems true in many East Asian societies (Table 6.4):

Corruption in Indonesia seems to have declined, but the Asia Political and Economic Risk Consultancy still rated in 2008 Indonesia as the most corrupt country in Asia. After democratization, money and mafia have infiltrated into Taiwanese politics, its democracy has been quickly monetized, and its top leader Chen Shui-bian embezzled so much that he landed himself in jail.[5] In South Korea, financial tycoons poured tons of money into presidential elections, and as for the Philippines, it is said that with each new government, it is the beginning of a new round of corruption.

Third, the economy is negatively affected. Thailand's economy has been hit hard by the constant political turmoil and street fights. The Philippines has adopted the American political model for nearly one century, but one third of its population is still mired in poverty. Mongolia

---

[5] Zhang Weiwei, "台湾民主的困境及其对两岸关系的影响" (Taiwan's Democracy Dilemma and Its Implications for Cross-Strait Relations", 《中国评论月刊》 (China Review Monthly), 11 (2007).

relies on the export of a few resources, and lags perhaps 20 years behind China's Inner Mongolia. South Korea was one of the largest victims of the 1997 Asian financial crisis and the ongoing financial tsunami. Taiwan under Chen Shui-bian performed poorly with insufficient public investments for eight years running. If South Korea has moved out of the crisis thanks to its close engagement with the fast-expanding Chinese market, Taiwan under Ma Ying-jeou is now trying to do the same as an effective way to move out of its economic downturn.

Thai opposition leader Lim Kit Siang, who initiated the democratization movement in Thailand in 1998, has now observed that Thai politics is extremely corrupt, country folks "extremely ignorant" and election has become "meaningless". He even proposed the parliamentary election to be replaced by appointment, as election in Thailand has "little meaning". Thailand adopted monarchical democracy back in 1932 but has since experienced 24 coup d'états.[6] Indonesia is now a democracy by Western standards, but its politics is still strongly influenced by powerful military and political families. My own estimate is that with some luck, Indonesia may become a low-quality democracy similar to India, and without such luck, it may eventually plunge into constant chaos, if not disintegration.

Japan belongs to a separate category, as it became modernized and a colonial power on a par with the West after the Meiji Restoration in the 1860s under imperial rule until its destruction at the end of the Second World War. Its democracy was imposed by the United States after the War, and it is now experiencing a two-decade-long recession, with few prime ministers serving more than a year. Most Japan watchers today ask the same question raised by a *Newsweek* lead article in 2009 about "Japan's lost leaders" and "Japan's leadership deficits" in this time of crisis.[7] This is not only a prolonged economic recession, but also a political systemic crisis, which is now compounded by the 2011 earthquake and nuclear plant disaster.[8]

The poor record of the Western model in East Asia reminds us of the need to explore political systems appropriate to one's cultural traditions.

---

[6] Hannah Beech, "Why Democracy is Struggling in Asia," *Time Magazine*, January 12, 2009, p. 30.

[7] Richard J. Samuels, "Japan's Lost Leaders", *Newsweek*, April 20, 2009.

[8] Michael Schuman, "The Japan Syndrome", *Time Magazine*, October 31, 2011.

East Asian societies, despite their different stages of development, seem to demonstrate some similar patterns of cultural traditions as well as some shared values, which include a stress on the community rather than the individual, the primacy of order and harmony over other considerations, an emphasis on hard work, saving and thriftiness, a belief that government and business need not necessarily be natural adversaries, and an emphasis on the role of the family.

In other words, culture matters a lot. The 2001–2003 East Asian Barometer Surveys offer some insights into the impact of culture on people's behavior in East Asian societies (Table 6.5). To my mind, if a political system fails to reflect these cultural values, it is bound to experience setbacks and failures.

David Hitchcock's 1994 survey of the value preferences of officials, business people, scholars and professionals from the United States and eight East Asian societies also contains interesting findings with regard to the priorities of values in the minds of different peoples: a strong majority of Asian respondents pick an orderly society and harmony as their top two values, which are almost alien to most Americans, while the Americans' top two values are freedom of speech and individual rights (Table 6.6).

In our effort to develop modern political systems in East Asia, due recognition must be given to these values, and to the need to ground these systems in Asia's specific cultural conditions. Otherwise, these societies are bound to encounter setbacks and failures as mentioned earlier.

The Chinese experience since 1978 shows that the ultimate test of a good political system is whether it can deliver good governance and a higher level of satisfaction for its people. As I have said earlier, good governance can take the form of the Western political system or non-Western political system, and bad governance can also take the form of the Western political system or non-Western political system. Each nation should explore its own political system appropriate to its conditions with the aim of achieving good governance.

In this vein of thought, some observations made by David Gosset, a French Sinologist, merit attention:

> The common and vivid Chinese locution "*jing di zhi wa*", or the frog
> at the bottom of the well, is used to deride a mix of parochialism,

Table 6.5   Impact of traditional values in East Asia

	Hong Kong	Taiwan	Japan	Philippines	Korea	China	Thailand	Mongolia	Average
For the sake of family, the individual should put his personal interests second.	90.2	86.1	72.7	79.0	69.9	91.0	88.1	73.6	81.3
If there is a quarrel, we should ask an elder to resolve the dispute.	36.9	68.9	66.2	75.8	44.2	72.4	76.7	70.9	64.0
When one has a conflict with a neighbour, the best way to deal with it is to accommodate the other person.	67.1	46.1	75.4	45.8	71.4	71.9	50.7	82.3	63.8
A person should not insist on his own opinion if his co-workers disagree with him.	53.4	63.0	61.4	57.0	61.4	51.6	62.3	66.7	59.6

Source: 2001–2003 East Asian Barometer Surveys.

Table 6.6   Priorities of values in East Asia and the United States

East Asia	The United States
1. Social harmony	Freedom of speech
2. Harmony	Individual rights
3. Accountability	Individual freedoms
4. Openness to new ideas	Public debate
5. Freedom of speech	Accountability

Source: David Hitchcock, *Asian Values and the United States: How Much Conflict?*, Center for Strategic and International Studies, Washington, DC, 1994.

narrow-mindedness and complacency. In an increasingly interconnected and interdependent global village, the expression does not apply to China. In a 2009 survey conducted by the Washington DC-based Pew Research Center, it appears that 93% of the Chinese respondents had a good opinion of international trade. The same institute estimates that 88% of the Chinese believe that their country's economic situation is good (17% for the US, 14% for France and 10% for Japan). In the Chinese collective psyche, opening-up, progress and confidence reinforce each other. The conjunction of these characteristics partly explains why the visitor to Beijing, Shanghai or Chongqing is often astonished by the energy which circulates, indeed, in most Chinese megalopolis.

In 2009, the Pew Center inquired about the level of satisfaction in 25 nations and the study shows that 87% of the Chinese are satisfied with the way things are going in their country (36% for the US, 27% for France and 25% for Japan). Any reflection on China's political system, economy, business or diplomacy has to integrate this high level of confidence in sharp contrast with the general apprehension which dominates in the Western countries.

The Chinese people's intense interest for the world does not mean that they forget or reject their own tradition. On the contrary, for most of the Chinese intellectuals or the Chinese global citizens, the opening up to foreign cultures is an invitation to the reinterpretation of China's tradition. In fact, China's curiosity for the outside world is concomitant with a return to the Chinese tradition and a reflection on the idea of "Chineseness". Can the West open itself to a Chinese renaissance as China opens itself to the world? If the West believes that it has nothing to learn from China, from its ancient wisdom, aesthetics, values, if the West, facing the overall success of the Chinese model, refuses to question its own assumptions about economic and political modernity, it simply takes the risk to end up as the last frog in the well.[9]

---

[9] David Gosset, "Who will be the Last Frog in the Well?", *Asia Times Online*, November 9, 2009.

Rather than lecturing China all the time, it is perhaps in the US's own interest to first of all put its own house in order and reflect more on why the financial crash originated in the US, causing havoc for the American and other peoples of the world, what the political and systemic causes of the crisis are, and why the American public is losing confidence in the American institutions. Indeed, American public trust in American politics and government today have hit an all-time low, as shown in the latest findings of the 2011 Gallup governance survey:

- 57 percent of Americans lack confidence in the federal government's ability to solve domestic problems.
- 69 percent have no confidence in Congress, an all-time high.
- The public thinks Washington wastes 51 cents of every tax dollar.
- Nearly half believe "the federal government has become so large and powerful that it poses an immediate threat to the rights and freedoms of ordinary citizens."[10]

It is reasonable to conclude that there is a fundamental breach of trust that goes beyond the Americans' habitual distrust of the government. People question the state capacity to forge a consensus on tackling effectively national problems. China has indeed done better in this regard thanks to its constant reforms since 1978, and Western democracy from Iceland to Greece to Britain to the United States is indeed in crisis. It is high time to question and fix the deep-seated problems of the political model developed in the West. But whatever happens in the West, China should continue to work hard to tackle well the problems and challenges on its way forward.

6.3 Debating with Fukuyama: The End of the End of History

Professor Francis Fukuyama, the author of the controversial book *The End of History and the Last Man*, was in Shanghai in mid-2011. The soft-spoken Japanese-American scholar gave a public lecture on June 27 on the China model and his new book *The Origins of Political Order* at the

---

[10] Will Marshall, "Democracy in Crisis", Progressive Policy Institute, September 29, 2011.

prestigious Wenhui Forum hosted by the Chunqiu Institute and Shanghai's *Wenhui Daily*, and his presentation was followed by a debate with me on a number of issues relating to the China model and the rise of China. As the debate has covered a wide range of topics contained in this book, I think it is only befitting to present it here, in part as a summary of my major arguments in this book and in part as additional food for thought for those who want to go further in reflecting on the relevance of the China model in the world today. My key argument, as readers of this book may discern by now, is that with the rise of China, its model of development and political discourse, it is not the end of history, but the end of the end of history.

Zhang: Prof. Fukuyama, in your presentation and new book, you've raised a number of issues concerning the China model, especially accountability, the rule of law, the "bad emperor" problem and sustainability. I would like to respond one by one. I think what China has been doing is very interesting, and China is perhaps now the world's largest laboratory for political, economic, social and legal reforms. What you've said reminds me of my dialogue with the editor-at-large of German magazine *Die Zeit* last February. The topic was also the China model. After his recent visit to Shanghai, he feels that there are more and more similarities between Shanghai and New York. In his eyes, China seems to follow the US model. "Does it mean that there is no China model, but only the US model?" I counseled him to look at Shanghai more carefully, as I am from Shanghai and know the city well. I told him that a more careful observer would find that Shanghai had overtaken New York in many aspects.

Shanghai outperforms New York in terms of "hardware", such as high-speed trains, subways, airports, harbors and many commercial facilities, and in terms of "software", for instance, life expectancy in Shanghai is three to four years longer than in New York, the infant mortality rate in Shanghai is lower, and Shanghai is a much safer place where girls can stroll on the streets at midnight. My message to this German scholar is that we've learnt a lot from the West, we're still learning from the West, and will continue to do so in the future, but it's also true that we have indeed looked beyond the Western model or the US model. To a certain extent, we are exploring the political, economic, social and legal systems of the next generation. In this process, the more developed regions of China like Shanghai are taking the lead. Now I would like to share my views on your doubts over the China model.

First, with regard to accountability, what you've discussed is the multi-party parliamentary democracy in the West. Having lived in the West for over two decades, I feel more than ever that this political accountability can hardly be effective. Frankly speaking, from my point of view, the American political system is rooted in the pre-industrialization era, and the need for political reform in the US is as strong as in China, if not more. The separation of powers within the political domain alone can no longer effectively address the major problems in the American society today; it has certainly failed to prevent the recent financial crisis.

To my mind, a modern society may need a new type of checks and balances, a balance between political, social and capital powers beyond the political domain. The separation of powers in the US has its weakness. As you said, many vested interest groups, such as the so-called military-industrial complex (or the power of capital in general), will not have their interests encroached upon, thus blocking many reform initiatives that are necessary for the US.

I think the accountability that the Chinese are exploring covers far wider areas than that in the US. China's experiment in this regard covers a whole range of economic, political and legal areas. For example, our government at all levels has the mission of promoting economic growth and job creation. An official cannot be promoted unless this mission is fulfilled. I read an article written by Paul Krugman, the Nobel Laureate in economics, in which he said that economic growth and job creation were zero in the past decade in the US. I think there is no place in China, any province, city or county, in the past two decades that has ever registered such a poor record. On the contrary, the economic performance across China is impressive. This is attributable to the Chinese practice of economic accountability. Of course, we have our own problems.

It is the same case with political and legal accountability. For example, we are now having our dialogue here in the Jing'an district of Shanghai, which is one of the best districts in Shanghai. Without exaggeration, it outperforms Manhattan in many ways in terms of both "hardware" and "software". But there was a fire accident last year that burned down a residential building in this district. As a result, 20 or so government officials and corporate executives were punished for their negligence of duties or malpractice. Such is the reality of China's political and legal accountability.

In contrast, the financial crisis in the US has made American citizens lose one fifth to one quarter of their assets, but after three years, nobody in the US has been held accountable politically, economically or legally. To make things worse, those financiers who are perhaps the culprits of the financial crisis are financially rewarded with tens or even hundreds of millions of dollars. However furious the American public and President Obama are, the bonuses are still awarded to them according to the contracts they signed in the name of the rule of law.

This reminds me of the second issue concerning the rule of law in the China model raised by you. We are promoting the rule of law in China and there is indeed huge room for improvement when it comes to the rule of law in China. But I think some elements of our traditional philosophy remain valid and relevant. For example, there is the traditional concept of *tian* or the heaven, which means the core interest and conscience of Chinese society. This can by no means be violated. Laws may be applied strictly to 99.9% of cases in China but we maintain a small space where political solutions, within the framework of the rule of law, are applied when *tian* or the core interest and conscience of the society are violated. In other words, the aforementioned Wall Street bonus issue would not happen in China. So we try to strike a balance between the rule of law and *tian*, and this is what China wants to do in its exploration of the legal regime of the next generation. Otherwise it is very likely to fall prey to what's called *fatiaozhuyi* or excessive legalism, which could be very costly for a huge and complex country like China.

As for the "bad emperor" issue, it has been solved. To say the least, my rough estimate is that even during the times of "good and bad emperors" in China's long history, there were at least seven dynasties which were longer than 250 years, in other words, longer than the entire history of the US. In fact, the entire contemporary history of the West is only about 200–300 years long and this history has witnessed slavery, fascism, tons of conflicts and two world wars. Nobody can guarantee that the current Western system will be sustainable. We may dwell on this later.

In my view, China's political institutional innovation has solved the issue of the "bad emperor". First and foremost, China's top leadership is selected on merit, and is not hereditary. Second, the term of office is strict and top leaders serve a maximum of two terms. Third, collective leadership is practiced, which means no single leader can prevail if he deviates too much from the group consensus. Last but not least, meritocracy-based selection is a time-honored tradition in China, and top-level decision-makers or members of the Standing Committee of the Political Bureau of the Communist Party of China are selected by criteria that usually include two terms as provincial governors or ministers. As you know, it is by no means easy to govern a Chinese province which is usually the size of four to five European countries. This system may have its weaknesses, but one can be certain that with this system of meritocracy, it is highly unlikely that China will elect a national leader as incompetent as George W. Bush or Naoto Kan of Japan. In fact, what concerns me now is not the "bad emperor" issue in China; rather it's the "George W. Bush" issue in the US. If the American political system continues as it is today, I am really concerned that the next elected US president will be even less competent than George W. Bush. As a superpower, the US's policies have global implications. So a lack of political leadership or accountability in the US could cause serious problems. I would like to have your view on the "George W. Bush" issue. Bush did not run his country well and the US declined sharply for eight years running. Even a country like the US cannot afford another eight years of further decline.

With regard to the sustainability of the China model, in my new book, I have put forward the concept of China as a unique civilizational state, which has its own logic and cycles of development, and the idea of dynasties is helpful here. A good dynasty in China tends to last 200–300 years or more, and this logic has been observed in the past 4,000 years. From this perspective, China now is still at the early stage of its current upward cycle. This is one reason I am optimistic about the future of China, and this has also been my view over the past two decades.

My optimism also comes from the Chinese concept of *shi* or overall trend, which is hard to be reversed once it takes hold. The course of development took a sharp turn in Japan thanks to the Meiji Restoration in the late 19th century while China didn't manage to do it due to China's strong internal inertia, which is a negative way of saying *shi*. Now a new *shi* or overall trend has taken hold and gained a strong momentum after the three-decade-long reform and opening up. This overall trend can hardly be reversed despite the fact that some waves may go in the opposite direction. It is the *shi* that defines the general trend of China's big cycles. Unfortunately many Western scholars fail to understand that, and their pessimistic predictions about China's collapse have lasted for about two decades, but instead of China collapsing, these predictions have "collapsed". Some Chinese within China still hold this pessimistic view. But I think this view will also "collapse", and that won't take another 20 years.

You mentioned the trade dependency of the China model. China indeed depends a lot on foreign trade, but this dependency has been somehow inflated. Foreign trade takes a large share of GDP if calculated based on the official exchange rate. But foreign trade is calculated in US dollars, and the rest of the GDP is calculated in the undervalued RMB. As a result, from my point of view, the trade dependency is exaggerated. Looking ahead, China's domestic demand may well become the world's largest. China's urbanization didn't gather pace until 1998. From now on, there will be 15–25 million new urban dwellers every year in China. This unprecedented scale of urbanization in human history will create immense domestic demand, which may be larger than the combined demand of all the developed countries in the future.

In terms of respecting individual values, I don't think there is a huge difference between China and the rest of the world. The end is the same, which is to respect and protect individual values and rights. But the difference lies in the means to achieve this end. China has a holistic tradition in contrast to the individualistic one in the West. In my view, the Chinese approach based on a holistic tradition produces better results in promoting individual values and rights. I describe the Chinese holistic approach as Deng Xiaoping's approach and India's individualistic approach as Mother Teresa's approach. Deng Xiaoping's approach has helped lift over 400 million Chinese individuals out of poverty and fulfilled their values and rights: they can watch color TVs, drive on highways and surf and blog on the Internet to comment on all kinds of subjects. But in India, although the Mother Teresa's approach touched and moved countless individuals and she was even awarded the Nobel Peace Prize, the overall picture of poverty in India remains largely unchanged.

I would also like to talk about public participation in the decision-making process. Actually I do hope that you will have the opportunity to do more field research in China. What is the Chinese way of democratic decision-making? Let me share with you an example. In China, we make a national development plan every five years. This is the crystallization of tens of thousands of rounds of discussions and consultations at all levels of the Chinese state and society. In my opinion, this is the real democratic decision-making process, and it ensures quality decision-making. The gap between the West and China in this regard is, to be frank, huge — to my mind, China is perhaps at the "graduate" level, and the West perhaps at the "undergraduate" or even "high school" level, if this analogy fits.

The recent turmoil in the Middle East, at first glance, is about the pursuit of freedom. But one of the root causes, to my mind, is the economy. I have been to Cairo four times. Twenty years ago, the city was about five years behind Shanghai. But now the difference is four decades. Half of the young generation is unemployed. Other than revolting, what can they do? My observation of the Middle East has led me to conclude that, while many in the West cheer the Arab Spring, one shouldn't be too optimistic. I hope the region will do well, but it will be difficult, and the Arab Spring today may well turn into an Arab Winter in a not-too-distant future with the American interest undermined. The situation in this region is no better than that of China during the 1911 Republican Revolution which was followed by chaos for a long time. There remains a long journey to go in the Middle East. We shall wait and see what will happen.

Fukuyama: Thank you for raising so many questions. Let me respond one by one. First of all, when you are comparing political systems, I think you should distinguish between policies and institutions. That is to say, the specific policies taken by certain leaders and the system as a whole. It is clear that American policy-makers made a lot of mistakes, for example, the Iraq War for which we paid a big price. And the financial crisis which originated from Wall Street, to some extent, is the result of the free market ideology, excessive household consumption and expansion in the property market. But policy mistakes can be made by any regime at any time. I don't think democratic regimes are more prone to policy mistakes than authoritarian ones. In fact, the latter have even bigger troubles. The mistakes could drag on as the decision-makers cannot be removed. So the price at the end of the day will be very high.

You said that China would never select a national leader like George W. Bush. Well, it is a bit hard to say that. George W. Bush was the president only for eight years. If you go back to the "bad emperor" problem, the last "bad emperor" China had, quite frankly, was Mao Zedong because the damage during the Cultural Revolution upon Chinese society was far more severe than anything George W. Bush did to American society. You also mentioned several characteristics of the Chinese leadership. What I want to say is that I do recognize the positive sides of collective leadership and the term limit in China. If Gaddafi or Mubarak had a term limit, they would not be in trouble.

You also said that consensus should be reached within the leadership in order to make important decisions. In my opinion, this practice is exactly a lesson learned from the Cultural Revolution. In the past, the happiness and anger of an individual wreaked havoc upon the whole society. So the Communist Party had to create new institutions which included a term limit. This is one of the reasons that I want to give credit to the Chinese system. Many Americans fail to recognize the fact that although China is an authoritarian country, it is also highly institutionalized and has checks and balances in its system. However, I think we need to think about the long run.

The current institutional setup within the Chinese Communist Party is based on the living memory of those who lived through the Cultural Revolution. It is not possible to talk about that part of the history fully in China. You are not teaching the younger generation what happened. They have not experienced the Cultural Revolution and tend to forget about it. The problem is what will happen if the new generation has no such experience and psychological scars from living under that kind of unconstrained dictatorship. Are they willing to live with the current checks on the use of power?

That is why I believe the formal rule of law and checks and balances in the long run are viable because they are not just reliant on the memory of one generation. If the next generation doesn't have the same memory, they might repeat the same mistakes. So I think the rule of law and democracy are the means to maintain what is good at the moment and let it transcend generations. This is for further elaboration on the "bad emperor" problem. To this, I want to go back to Chinese history.

In my new book, one of the things that I argue is that we all have a common human nature. That human nature makes us favor our families, friends, brothers, sisters and children especially. Giving our personal preference to friends is a kind of natural mode of human social interaction. But we cannot base political systems on friends and families. So one of the greatest achievements of Chinese politics is to create a political system that is highly institutionalized beyond all friends and families, beyond kinship and personal relations.

So in order to get into bureaucracy, you have to take exams. It is not just based on who is relatively influential. This system was fully institutionalized in the earlier Han Dynasty in the 1st century BC. But at the end of the late Han Dynasty in the 3rd century, the political system was recaptured by the elite, basically by families who had a lot of wealth and power. Then there was the period of the Three Kingdoms which was a very complicated period of Chinese history. Basically rich families recaptured power and the very modern institution deteriorated. I think this could happen to any political system. In some respects, this is something I am worried about in the American system because we have the elite who are very wealthy. They can take care of their children well and send them to very good schools. Of course this is not what is happening in China, but can be a threat in the Chinese system.

How do you make sure that the elite who run the country remain to be based on merit and talent, as opposed to families and friends? I would say, the Communist Party of China in the past few decades has done a very good job. However, there is corruption in the whole system. People want to take care of their relatives, friends and children. I think one of the problems in a system without downward political accountability is that sometimes it is hard to prevent the re-entry of these personal connections into the political system. So again that is the problem I don't think has been really solved. In the long run, in order to let the system perpetuate for two or three decades, I believe we need downward accountability to solve the problem. I am not trying to defend everything that goes on in the US. I grew up in New York City and I know there are a lot of crimes and things are not working so well in many respects. But at least in a democratic system, we make mistakes and we recover from them. And it sometimes takes quite a number of years.

Let me quickly talk about one observation about the US. We have experienced the financial crisis. As you said, nobody has been punished. I think that is terrible because we have not held accountable people who are responsible for the financial crisis. Why it happened is complicated. But I don't think it has to do with our democratic political system because in the 1930s we had an even bigger economic crisis and it led to the election of President Roosevelt and an entirely new welfare state and regulatory system. They took a lot of strong measures because people were angry about what had happened. So the system can produce real accountability in the face of big policy mistakes. So in some sense, I even think the problem in the last couple of years in the US is that this crisis is not big enough. So policy-makers actually in a way mitigated the crisis. So the political momentum that favors reform is kind of undermined. That is why we didn't get adequate regulatory reform. But I don't think our democratic system caused the current crisis.

Zhang: I can respond briefly to what you've just said. I think each country has ugly events or mistakes in its history, including China. The Cultural Revolution and Great Leap Forward were indeed tragedies. I have my own personal experience of the Cultural Revolution. But it is necessary to emphasize that no country is an exception. The US has a history of slavery and Indian massacres, and institutionalized racial discrimination lasted for over a century. You think that mistakes are corrected by the American system itself. Likewise, the Cultural Revolution and Great Leap Forward were also corrected by the Chinese system itself. The "bad emperor" issue has been solved by the Chinese system. Now it is unlikely that any single leader can reverse the institutional setup because what has taken shape in China is a system of power transfer that combines selection with some kind of election. I think this hybrid model is probably better than the pure election in the West, especially from the perspective of exploring the next generation's political system.

What the West is practicing is increasingly an election system which I sometimes call "showbiz democracy" or "Hollywood democracy", and it's more about showmanship than leadership. As long as the procedure is right, it doesn't matter who is elected, be it a movie star or a professional athlete, whereas in the Chinese tradition of political governance, there is a very important idea, i.e. the country can only be run by people with talent and expertise selected on meritocracy. This is deeply rooted in the Chinese mind.

You mentioned Chairman Mao. On the one hand, it's true that he made serious mistakes. On the other hand, we should not neglect the fact that he is still widely respected in China, and this shows Mao must have done something right, and it is not fair to deny his main achievements, which include, first, unifying a country as large as China; second, women's liberation; and third, land reform. Deng Xiaoping once said Chairman Mao's achievements outweighed his mistakes 70% to 30%. I myself heard him making this comment, and I think it's a fair assessment. Perhaps this different perception of Mao has to do with the different cultural traditions: the Chinese have a tradition of political dynamics while the West legal dynamics. Thanks to the three-decade reform and opening up, there has emerged a stable middle class. I divide the Chinese society into three layers: upper, middle and lower. This structure can prevent the large-scale extremism of the Mao era. Such extremism is still possible in countries like Egypt because of the lack of a middle stratum. This is the structural reason China is not likely to shift towards extremism.

With respect to corruption, I think we need to make what can be called "vertical" and "horizontal" comparisons. Corruption in China is serious and not all that easy to tackle. However, reviewing world history, you will find that all major powers including the US experienced periods of rising corruption, which often coincided with the process of rapid modernization. As your teacher Prof. Samuel Huntington observed, the fastest process of modernization is often accompanied by the fastest-rising corruption. This is mainly due to the fact that the regulatory and supervisory regimes simply cannot catch up with the growth of wealth and capital in times of rapid modernization. Eventually corruption in China will be tackled and solved through the establishment of better regulatory and supervisory institutions.

I have visited the US on many occasions and found that the definition of corruption matters a lot. In my new book, I put forward a concept of the "second generation of corruption", as the financial crisis has exposed many serious "second generation of corruption" issues. For instance, rating agencies gain profits through regulatory arbitrage by granting triple A's to dubious financial products or institutions. I think this is corruption. But these issues are called "moral hazards" in the American legal system. I think the financial crisis could be better tackled if these problems were treated as corruption.

We can also make horizontal comparisons. I have visited more than 100 countries. The reality is that no matter how much the Chinese are complaining about corruption at home, it is much worse in other nations of comparable size, say, those with a population of 50 million and above, and at a similar stage of development, such as India, Ukraine, Pakistan, Brazil, Egypt and Russia. The evaluation of Transparency International echoes my view. As a civilizational state, China is an amalgamation of "hundreds of states into one" over its long history and this kind of state cannot apply the Western political system without risking its own breakup.

Furthermore, it's necessary to look at such a large country as China in terms of regions. China's developed regions are more immune to corruption. I once stayed in Italy as a visiting professor and visited Greece several times, and I think Shanghai is definitely less corrupt than Italy and Greece. In southern Italy, even the Mafia has been de facto legalized through the democratic system. I first went to Greece more than 20 years ago when its fiscal deficit was high. Now Greece is bankrupt and needs assistance. I said to my Greek friend very frankly: "Twenty years ago, your prime minister was Papandreou. Twenty years later, your prime minister is still Papandreou, and your politics seems to be a few families' business, and the Greek economy has gone bankrupt as a result of an excessively high welfare system and poor governance." I joked once that we could send a team from Shanghai or Chongqing to help Greece with good governance. Indeed, whatever the political system, be it a one-party system, multi-party system or no-party system, it must all boil down to good governance and what you can deliver to your people. Therefore, good governance matters most, rather than Western-style democratization.

This brings me to your "end of history" thesis. My view is exactly the opposite of yours. I take the view that it is not the end of history, but the end of the end of history. The Western democratic system might be only transitory in the long history of mankind. Why do I think so? Two thousand and five hundred years ago, some Greek city-states like Athens practiced democracy among its male citizens, and later they were defeated by Sparta.

From then on, for over 2,000 years, the word "democracy" basically carried a negative connotation in Europe, often equivalent to "mob politics". The Western countries did not introduce the one-person-one-vote system into their countries until their modernization process was completed.

But today, this kind of democratic system cannot solve the following big problems. First, there is no culture of "talent first". Anyone who is elected can rule the country. This has become too costly and unaffordable even for a country like the US. Second, the welfare package can only go up, not down. Therefore it is impossible to launch such reforms as what China did to its banking sector and state-owned enterprises. Third, it is getting harder and harder to build a social consensus within their countries. In the past, the winning party with 51% of the votes could unite the whole society in the developed countries. Today, even the American society is deeply divided and polarized. The losing party, instead of conceding defeat, continues to obstruct. Fourth, there is an issue of simple-minded populism which means that little consideration can be given to the long-term interest of a nation and society. Even countries like the US are running this risk.

In 1793, King George III of the UK sent his envoy to China to open bilateral trade. But Emperor Qianlong of China was so arrogant that he believed China was the best country in the world. Therefore China did not need to learn anything from others. This is what defined the "end of history" then, and ever since then China began to decline. Now I observe a similar mindset in the West. It's necessary to come to China and see with one's own eyes how China has reformed itself over the past three decades. Small is each step, yet the journey is non-stop. The West still has strong faith in its own system, but it is the same system that has become more and more problematic. Greece, the cradle of Western democracy, has gone bankrupt. British debt is as high as 90% of its GDP. The Chinese Premier is on an official visit to the UK today with the intention of making some investment there, and the British are very happy about this. What about the US? I did a simple calculation. The 9/11 attack cost the US about US$1 trillion, the two not-so-smart wars cost the US about US$3 trillion and the financial crisis about US$8 trillion. Now the fiscal debt of the US is somewhere between US$10 to US$20 trillion. In other words, if the US dollar were not the main international reserve currency — this status may not last forever — the US might have gone bankrupt already.

I have a friend who immigrated to the US from Shanghai a decade ago. If he had chosen to stay in Shanghai and bought a property or made some investment in China like just about everyone else, his wealth would have increased two- to three-fold. Now the US is mired in a financial crisis. He suffered a great loss from purchasing US dollars with the RMB due to the dollar's depreciation, and the financial crisis further cut his assets in the US by one quarter. So in the end, it is difficult for him to return to Shanghai now. The rise of China is what we call *shi* or an overall trend, the scale and speed of which is unprecedented in human history. My own feeling is that the Western system is trekking on a downward slope and in need of major repair and reform.

Fukuyama: Again I want to say that you need to distinguish political system from short-term policy. So it is no question that the US, in the past generation, has had excessive borrowing. But I actually don't think this is the problem of our democratic system. Germany is very much close to China. It is a large economy that carries a consistent trade surplus and a relatively booming job market. At the same time, Germany is not obsessed with the excessive financial innovation that brought down the US economy and caused the property bubble. It is a democratic country. It has just made choices different from the US. So I don't think it has anything to do with whether this country is a democracy or not. Every country can make policy mistakes.

Again I want to put things into perspective. I really don't want to belittle the great achievement that China has scored. However, my point is that you cannot make long-term judgment according to short-term performance. Japan was unstoppable in the late 1980s before the bursting of the Japanese property bubble. After the bubble burst and following policy mistakes, there was 20 years of economic stagnation and low growth. But people in the mid-1980s believed that Japan would grow larger and larger until it overtook the US. There was a belief of emerging Japanese supremacy. Now I think if you look at economic growth from a longer-term perspective, what is the bigger challenge for China is the same for any economy. There is a period of really rapid economic growth and industrialization will mobilize people from the countryside to cities.

Europe grew rapidly at that stage, so did Korea and Japan. Perhaps 25 years ago, China entered this process. At a certain point, that transition got people out of the agricultural economy. Then you face the next challenge of productivity in a more mature economy. And I think it is probably a universal truth that no country has ever maintained double-digit growth up to the point where you have become an industrialized economy. That will happen to China as well. The Chinese economy will slow down in the next generation. All countries, in particular Asian countries, will face this problem because the birth rate is coming down which is going to be a huge burden. The elderly population is large because of greater longevity and low infant mortality, not the one-child policy. So this is true in Taiwan, Singapore and mainland China. I attended a meeting this morning. One of the economists said that in the year of 2040 or 2050, China is going to have 400 million people over 60 years old. That is an enormous challenge that other developed countries face as well. So when we talk about the resilience of the political system, we have to think about the long term. Given the different upcoming challenges of a falling birth rate and a much older population, how flexible can the system be? But I would not say that democratic countries have all the answers. This is a challenge for everyone.

Professor Zhang also brought up the issue of populism which means in democracies people do not always make the right choices. I think there are many examples of this in American politics these days. Sometimes I have to shake my head because of some stupid decisions made by politicians. But Abraham Lincoln, I think the greatest president of the US, has a famous saying: "You can fool some of the people all of the time, and all of the people some of the time, but you cannot fool all of the people all of the time." Particularly with the rise of education and income, I think this kind of populism in some respects has changed. This is a test of real democracy. Yes, people in the short run make bad decisions or choose the wrong leaders. But the thing is, in a mature democracy there is genuine freedom of expression and genuine ability to debate issues. In the long run, people will make the right decisions. I think in the history of the US, we can point out many bad short-term decisions, but in the end people will come to understand their interests in the long run which will lead them to make the right decisions.

Winston Churchill, the great British prime minister, once said: "Democracy is the worst form of government except for all those others that have been tried." I think it is important because the question is what you have as alternatives. The alternative is a really high-quality authoritarian government which I admit that China has had in the last generation. That may be a better system. But the question is how you guarantee that institution will guide the society to make the right decisions. Professor Zhang also mentioned the rise of a middle class. He said that this rules out the possibility of insurgency.

One of my teachers is Samuel Huntington. He wrote a book in 1968 called *Political Order in Changing Societies*. I was actually teaching that book at Stanford. One of the things that Samuel Huntington said is that revolutions are never created by poor people. They are actually created by middle-class people. They are created by people who are educated to have opportunities. But these opportunities are blocked by the political or economic system. It is the gap between their expectation and the ability of the system to accommodate their expectation which causes political instability. So the growth of a middle class, I think, is not a guarantee against insurgencies, but a cause of insurgencies.

What happened in Egypt and Tunisia was the growth of a fairly large middle class, a lot of college graduates and a lot of people who use the Internet. They are connected to the outside world and understand how bad their governments were. In terms of the sustainable growth of China, I actually don't think the force of China's instability will come from the poor peasants in the countryside. Political revolutions are introduced by the educated middle class because the current political system prevents them from being connected with the larger outside world and doesn't grant them the kind of social status that they deserve. I know there are 6–7 million new college graduates every single year in China. I think one of the greatest challenges to stability is not the poor people in China, but the middle class. Whether the society is capable of meeting their expectations, that is the question.

In terms of corruption, I don't want to argue that democracies can solve the question of corruption because obviously you have quite a few democracies with a high level of corruption. In many respects, China may be less corrupt than many of these democratic countries. But I do think that one way of combating corruption is freedom of press where you have the ability to expose corruption without being concerned about possible coercion or threats. True freedom of the press is an important tool against high-level corruption. In democratic countries, that doesn't always happen. For example in Italy, the prime minister owns the whole media. But I do think it is an advantage to have freedom of speech whereby you actually can criticize those powerful people in the political hierarchy and don't have to worry about personal retaliation. That is the advantage of having a liberal democratic system.

Zhang: Thank you, Prof. Fukuyama. You said that we should make evaluations in a longer timeframe. In 1985, I visited the US as an interpreter for a Chinese leader, and we met with Dr. Henry Kissinger. When he was asked to talk about Sino-US relations, he said he would rather listen to us first, because we came from a country of thousands of years of civilization. Of course this was a token of courtesy. However, we should remember the fact that China was indeed a more advanced country in terms of national strength and political system in most of the past 2,000 years. I do want to give credit to you, Prof. Fukuyama, for what distinguishes you from many other Western scholars is that you have spent a lot of time and effort studying the political institutions of ancient China as evidenced by your observation that China established the world's first modern state.

China lagged behind the West in the past 200–300 years. But China is catching up fast, particularly in the more developed regions. I am afraid that the West is a bit too arrogant and fails to look at China with an open mind. To my mind, the West can already learn something from China. President Obama may be right, as he urged the US to build high-speed railways, focus on basic education, reduce the fiscal deficit, have more savings, develop the manufacturing industry and drive up the export sector. He has kept emphasizing that the US cannot become the world's No. 2, and it is very obvious that he feels the pressure from the rise of China.

You sound optimistic on the issue of populism. You have great faith in the US that it can learn from its own mistakes, rather than being led by populism. But I tend to take the view that populism seems to be even more widespread in the world today thanks to the modern media. Now a country or society in fact may crash quickly because of excessive populism, and this is more than an issue of political institutions. Here is my argument. In

China, its thousands of years of traditions leave their mark on everything. I am not saying tradition is always good or bad. My point is that it is impossible or unrealistic to break from one's tradition as it always has an imprint on what we are doing today. Therefore I always say that like it or not, the Chinese characteristics are with us all the time because the Chinese historical genes are with us. What we can do is to leverage the advantages of our traditions while mitigating whatever disadvantages in our traditions. What happened in the Cultural Revolution tells us that it is very difficult to break from one's tradition. China does have some very good traditions which include belief in meritocracy, so selection plus some form of election offers a promising future for China, and we can do well in this regard, given our thousands of years of experience in meritocracy-based selection.

You talked about alternatives to democracy. This is exactly an area where our views differ. China does not have the intention to market its model as an alternative for other peoples or countries. What we focus on is simply running our own country well, which means doing a good job for one fifth of mankind, and nothing is better than achieving this goal. But it is also true that if you do well, others will follow your example. Today virtually all of China's neighboring countries, from Russia to India, from Vietnam, Laos, Cambodia to the Central Asian nations, are learning in one way or another from the China model.

Professor Huntington's view of the conflict between the middle class and the state is shared by most Western and some Chinese scholars who advocate an independent civil society. But China has its own long cultural traditions, which may affect China's middle class in a different way. Most Westerners view "government as a necessary evil", but most Chinese view "government as a necessary virtue". With this cultural legacy, the Chinese middle class is more likely to become the staunchest supporter of China's stability in the world as is the case now. In addition, instead of being confrontational, the relationship between the middle class and the Chinese state is most likely to be positively interactive, rather than confrontational. This will generate a social cohesion in the Chinese society perhaps unmatched in any Western society.

Now I would like to talk about the issue of corruption. We all know Asia's four Little Dragons: South Korea, Taiwan, Singapore and

Hong Kong. After their modernization process was largely completed, Taiwan and South Korea adopted the Western political system while Singapore and Hong Kong chose to stay more or less on the same course. Look at the situation today: Hong Kong and Singapore are much less corrupt than South Korea and Taiwan, as acknowledged by all those who study corruption. Hong Kong used to be very corrupt in the 1960s, but this problem was successfully tackled by setting up the Independent Commission Against Corruption (ICAC). In other words, the Western democratic system is by no means the best solution to the issue of corruption at least in the non-Western world. Transparency International's corruption indicators show that most non-Western "democracies" with a population of 50 million and above are faced with more corruption at home than China. As a matter of fact, corruption has become worse in Taiwan after it became a Western-style democracy. Otherwise Taiwan's leader Chen Shui-bian would not end up in jail. South Korea's five elected presidents were all implicated one after another in corruption scandals. In contrast, Hong Kong and Singapore, without adopting the Western political model, have succeeded in sharply reducing corruption through the rule of law and institutional innovation.

As for Churchill's remark about democracy, some Chinese rephrased his remark into "democracy is the least bad system". I checked the context of his remark and found that he made it in a Westminster debate in 1947, and he was clearly referring to the Western democracy as practiced in the West. Winston Churchill himself was firmly opposed to India's independence. How could he be expected to support India's adoption of Western democracy? But I myself have borrowed Winston Churchill's phrase and described the China model as "the least bad model", which means it has its weaknesses, but it has performed better than other models.

Fukuyama: Let me start with the question of the middle class. Is the Chinese middle class different from the middle class of non-Chinese societies? This is actually a question that I debated a lot with Professor Huntington. He wrote a book *The Clash of Civilizations* in 1990, in which he basically made the argument that culture determines behavior. You have certain major cultural systems such as Indian, Muslim, Christian and Confucian around the world. Despite the changes brought by modernization, culture still determines people's behavior even though they are more modern. I believe culture is very important. The reason I study international politics is that I like observing people who are different from me. If everyone in the world is the same as those I meet in Palo Alto or San Francisco, I would not have the interest to talk to people. So cultural diversity is the reality and it is good that not everybody is the same. But one of the larger questions is whether culture really projects itself across time in a way that resists the process of political, social and economic development or whether the process of modernization doesn't lead to a kind of cultural convergence.

Let me give you one example. Look around this room in which there are a lot of women sitting. Why are there a lot of women in the audience? In traditional times, the status of women was low in the societies where inheritance usually went to the male line and opportunities for women were very limited. It was true in the US and Europe at their early stage of development. But when you travel around the developed world and here in East Asia, you see women everywhere. Why is that the case? Why has women's status been raised? Why are they working in offices and factories? Why do they enjoy equal economic and social rights as men? The reason is the process of modernization. Some cultural nuisances about the appropriate roles of women now turn out to be wrong. A lot of people believed women couldn't compete with men in the workplace. They had the natural roles of only raising children and families, so on and so forth. But today you cannot run a modern economy without females in the labor force.

Saudi Arabia doesn't allow women to drive. So they have to employ around half a million chauffeurs from South Asia simply to drive their women around. If they didn't have oil, this would probably be the most insane economic system you could possibly imagine. Despite the Muslim culture about the appropriate roles of women, women in the Middle East are getting more powerful and more politically organized. They are demanding equal rights as men. This seems to me to be the case where different cultures come up with similar solutions to a problem which is the status of women. It happens not because culture is a determinant, but because the modernization process forces societies to come up with solutions. So I don't think you can have a modern society without granting equal rights to women. Of course this is an open question. Professor Zhang said that middle-class people who are educated, relatively secure and have private properties are going to be different from middle-class people else-where because they live in a Chinese cultural system. Maybe that is the case.

But from my observation, middle-class people in different cultures actually behave in similar ways. In the Arab world, people think the Arab people are different because they have Islam and they have different authorities. Yet through the past year only the Arab people have been on the street to demonstrate against their governments. So I think that some of the assumptions about what is culture may not be right. Maybe culture did dictate some behavior in the past. But under the current situation, it is different. With the Internet or travel, maybe people's behavior is deter-mined by the needs and aspirations of the current generation.

Let me say just one final thing on which I agree with Professor Zhang. I do think that there is a failure among the people in the US and Europe to appreciate Chinese achievement, both the contemporary and historical achievement. My recent book has six chapters, out of which three are on China. There are more chapters on China than other parts of the world. I really spent a lot of time trying to teach myself as much Chinese history as I could. I think that recognizing the strength of that history is important for Americans and also for Chinese. I think no civilization can live on bor-rowed values and institutions. So what I perceive is going on right now in China is an attempt to recover authentic Chinese roots. I think this is a good thing that China has to do. I think the challenge is to recover that pride in history and tradition and make it compatible with modern insti-tutions. We should do it in a way that doesn't lead to nationalism or nar-row chauvinism. What is a modern Japan like? It is not similar to the US, UK or France. It has rich Japanese characteristics. I think a modern China needs to have very Chinese characteristics as well. So it is going to be a very important task to figure out what are typical Chinese characteristics and what is required of a modern society. That is also part of a larger interna-tional order. Only in this way can we live with others peacefully.

Zhang: Let me make a brief response. Many Western political scientists take the view that modernization leads to cultural convergence. But expe-rience proves that it is not necessarily true. Let's take China as an example. The Chinese are known to be busy with modernization, creating wealth and making money these years. But a few years ago, a song became an instant national hit that encouraged people to visit their parents more often. This song is heart-warming to most Chinese and it struck a chord with the public. In other words, despite the rapid pace of modernization and the rise of individualism, at the core of the Chinese tradition is still family, for which most Chinese are willing to make much more sacrifices than most Westerners. My point is that the very essence of a culture is unlikely to be changed and will not be changed by modernization. Otherwise the world would become too boring. How can it be possible to change the essence of a culture as strong as China's? One is the McDonald's culture, and the other is China's eight-schools-of-cuisine culture, and they are immensely different. Indeed, the former has no power to conquer the latter. Rather, the latter may be able to assimilate the former. I appreciate the views of Edmund Burke, a British political philosopher of the 19th century, who held that any change in a political system must be derived mainly from a nation's own traditions.

Furthermore, I think, the main reason for respecting cultures is our respect for wisdoms associated with cultures. Wisdom and knowledge are two different things. We have far more knowledge today than any time in the past. Our school kids today may have more knowledge than Confucius or Socrates. However, human wisdom has hardly grown. Here I have a simple suggestion, which I'm not sure if you will accept: in addition to the three elements of a modern political institution you have mentioned, namely, state, accountability and the rule of law, we could add one more element, i.e. wisdom, as I have observed that the US has won many wars tactically, but lost them strategically, such as the wars in Vietnam, Afghanistan and Iraq, to name just a few. This situation has to do with wisdom, and I think the importance of wisdom can hardly be overemphasized.

I was recently in Germany to give a lecture. One German economist told me a story. German Chancellor Angela Merkel asked a German economist why there were no first-class economists or Nobel laureates in economics in Germany. This economist replied, "Mme Chancellor, please don't worry about this at all, because if there were first-class economists, there would be no first-class economy." In other words, it's economics that is in trouble. Among all social sciences invented in the West, I think economics is arguably the closest to truth because it is more like the natural sciences and supported by mathematical models. With this in mind, frankly speaking, political science and other social sciences invented in the West may well be further away from the truth than economics. This is why we should be bolder in our thinking and more courageous in our efforts for discourse innovations. I may share one commonality with you that we are both trying to work out of the box of Western political science, and your new book tries to integrate anthropology, sociology, economics, archeology and more. Your efforts merit our recognition and respect, though I don't agree with you on everything. On our part, my colleagues and I are indeed moving a bit further than you and we are questioning the whole range of the Western political discourse. But our intention is not to score political points or to prove how good China is or how bad the West is, or vice versa. Rather we try to leverage efforts to address such global challenges as poverty eradication, clashes of civilizations, climate change and various problems associated with urbanization. Western wisdom is indeed insufficient, and Chinese wisdom should make its contributions now.

At the end of this debate, I must admit a certain degree of triumphalism about the China model is tempting. But my intention is beyond that. Yes, China is rising fast, and most experts expect China to become the world's largest economy in 10 to 20 years, with a middle class twice the size of the whole US population, and the center of gravity seems shifting faster than expected since the global financial crisis in 2008. I have argued in this book that China's rise is not the rise of an ordinary country, but the rise of a country *sui generis*, a civilizational state, a new model of development and a new political discourse, and all this is bringing a wave of change unprecedented in human history.

But no one should get upset or hysterical. Just as economic growth is not a zero-sum game and others, especially the West, benefit from China's fast-expanding economy. Models of development and political ideas are not necessarily zero-sum games either, and they should not be perceived as such so we can all share a bit of the age-old Chinese wisdom of "selective learning and adaptation" and "harmony in diversity".

China has learnt so much from the West and will continue to do so for its own benefit. It may be time now for the West, to use Deng's famous phrase, to "emancipate the mind" and learn a little more about or even from China's approach and the Chinese ideas, however extraneous they may appear, for its own benefit. This is not only to avoid further ideology-driven misreadings of this hugely important nation, a civilization in itself, but also to enrich the world's collective wisdom in tackling challenges ranging from poverty eradication to job creation to climate change and the clash of civilizations.

At this time when the US and Europe are in crisis and the Anglo-Saxon model is perceived to be "in tatters" by many, all countries, the Western countries included, should engage in necessary reforms so as to better meet the expectations of their own people for good governance and better tackle the multiplying global challenges facing mankind today. It is in this context that one should be able to better appreciate China's continuous reforms since 1978, China's evolving model of development, the Chinese civilizational state and China's political discourse.

With the rise of China is an unprecedented wave of change in global economic and political arena, but this change, remarkable for China and the Chinese for sure, is not and should not be a zero-sum game. Rather it should be a win-win process for all, and it can be so as long as one keeps an open, broad and inclusive mind. In other words, it is not the end of history, but a win-win end of the end of history. History is unfolding in a fascinating way, which is good for China, for the West itself, for the rest of the world, and for the interest of all mankind.

INDEX

World Century Publishing Corporation is a joint venture in the United States formed by World Scientific Publishing Company and Shanghai Century Publishing Group. This collaboration draws on both our strengths to publish titles related to China's economy, society, and culture, including Traditional Chinese Medicine (TCM). World Century authors will consist of leading scholars and practitioners globally, including experts from within China. The books are distributed by World Scientific worldwide.

World Scientific, established in Singapore, is a leading independent international publisher in Science, Technology, Medicine, and Social Sciences. It has 9 offices worldwide and publishes more than 500 book titles a year and 120 journals for the academic and professional communities. Notably, World Scientific was awarded the exclusive rights to publish the Nobel Lectures in English, and it is also the exclusive distributor for The National Academies Press (United States) in Asia (except Japan).

Shanghai Century, established in China as the first publishing group approved by the Government, is one of the leading publishers in the country. Its publications range from higher education to mass-market titles. The group has since expanded to comprise more than 40 subsidiaries, including 29 book publishers, 8 audio-visual and electronic publishers, 72 journals and 8 newspapers.